KINGDOM-FOCUSED
FINANCES
for the Family

All Scripture quotations are taken from the KING JAMES VERSION.

ISBN: 978-1-936208-08-1

Layout and cover design: Lydia Zook
Front cover photos: istockphoto.com
Illustrations by Nathan Wright

Printed in the USA
First printing: September 2010
Second printing: November 2010

For more information about Christian Aid Ministries, see page 235

Published by:
TGS International
P.O. Box 355
Berlin, Ohio 44610 USA
Phone: 330·893·4828
Fax: 330·893·2305
www.tgsinternational.com

KINGDOM-FOCUSED
FINANCES
for the Family

A CALL TO BIBLICAL STEWARDSHIP

IN EVERYDAY LIFE

Gary Miller

Table of Contents

Introduction

We live in an age when time is of the essence. Everyone is in a hurry. New techniques and technology have transformed almost every industry, and tasks that once took our ancestors weeks, such as harvesting grain, can now be accomplished in a fraction of the time. Other jobs, such as plowing the soil, are being eliminated altogether.

Transportation has also changed tremendously. In one hour we can journey distances by airplane that would have taken our forefathers weeks or even months. We live in a world of instant accessibility. While those in the past had to wait months to hear from relatives on the other side of the Atlantic, we can pick up a telephone and within seconds converse with people all around the globe.

An Instant Society

We have grown accustomed to our instant society. Everything, it seems, is done instantly. Take a walk through the local grocery store and *instant* is the word of choice. No longer do you need to go to the cellar, scrub, peel, cook, mash, and clean up all the mess. Just add instant hot water from your dispenser at the sink, and there you have it—instant mashed potatoes. Want to add turkey to the menu? It waits for you in the prepared meat section, parked in its own oven-proof condo to maintain moisture, complete with a pop-up thermometer to ensure a perfect turkey every time, pre-seasoned for succulent taste, and ready to go with the easy-grip plastic handle on top. The list of instant items available to the cook who is willing to exchange a little quality and taste for time goes on and on. When dinner is over, just drop everything in the garbage can and cleanup is instantaneous as well.

Time

Time seems to be the theme of our age. No one wants to wait. From drive-through banking to overnight shipping, businesses advertise their ability to perform quickly. Our eating establishments are known as fast food, and patients needing surgical procedures that once required weeks in the hospital are now sent to same-day outpatient facilities. Someone defined a split second as "the time between when the light turns green and the fellow behind you honks." Everyone is in a hurry and preoccupied with efficiency and time.

The Effect

All this has had a profound effect on our generation. We think differently about tasks, food, and life itself. The resulting impact on our churches, homes, and young families cannot be overstated. We have come to expect instant results. We are no longer interested in waiting, and this change in our society has dovetailed nicely with our natural tendency toward impatience. Our society is telling us we should suffer silently no longer.

Is your marriage troubled? Get a divorce. There are lawyers who can do it quickly and efficiently. Having a struggle with your boss? Just move on and find another job. You shouldn't have to waste time doing things you don't want to do. Are your church leaders not leading like you think they should? Tell them what you think, and if things don't change immediately, plenty of other churches are out there. As our society and our lives have sped up, we have lost our ability to wait. If we can't get our Big Mac within three minutes, something is definitely wrong. We have lost the virtue of patience.

I Want It Now

Sadly, this trend and mindset has also trickled down into our finances. Whereas at one time couples started married life with few possessions and low expectations, couples now start out expecting to immediately have every material blessing their parents and grandparents have labored many years to obtain. Instead of slowly saving to purchase a new couch, car, or refrigerator, many couples expect to have all this and more as they begin their married life. Many of our young families expect to possess in three years what it has taken their parents thirty to accumulate.

But our young families need to understand something, and this is one of the burdens of this book.

> **Many of our young families expect to possess in three years what it has taken their parents thirty to accumulate.**

There are long-term consequences for immediate gratification. A young couple immediately requiring thirty years' worth of possessions will have problems. The only way this can occur, short of having a foolish, wealthy relative, is by accumulating consumer debt. Unfortunately, many lending institutions are all too willing to help us down this road to materialism and instant gratification, and unless our young families are taught and forearmed, they are likely to succumb to temptation.

In this book we want to look at the importance of developing a godly, Christ-centered vision for our homes and our finances. We want to examine how to create a financial road map that enables us to know where we are, where we want to go, and how we can get there from our present location. And last, we want to look at methods, a mindset that will help us stay on track, and the blessing of committing every part of our homes and lives, including our finances, to Jesus Christ.

The God of Mammon

Every culture has had its idols. Our culture is willingly sacrificing time, peace of mind, children, and sometimes even health on the altar of materialism. The chase is on for one more gadget, another antique, a nicer boat, a larger home, or a newer car. But in the midst of this mindless chase for more, God is calling us to come out and be separate. We are called to "love not the world, neither the things that are in the world."

Many American homes today are known as "Christian" homes. The occupants attend church each Sunday and verbally express their belief in Jesus. But just calling a brown barn red doesn't make the barn red. If we worship the world's idols and pursue the world's goals, the Bible says the love of the Father is not in us.

Why did Jesus focus so heavily on the subject of finance? Why is such a seemingly disproportionate amount of space in the Bible given to the use of money? There is more written on money and our use of it than almost any other topic. Jesus taught much more about money than heaven or hell, or even topics like evangelism and prayer. Jesus seemed preoccupied with the topic of wealth and materialism, and many times His words seem almost redundant. Why did Jesus place so much emphasis on money?

> **Jesus taught much more about money than heaven or hell, or even topics like evangelism and prayer.**

I think the answer is obvious, yet frequently ignored. What does wealth, or the "god of mammon," offer today? The god of mammon offers security, happiness, and acceptance by others. If you are willing to bow to the god of mammon, you are promised the abundant life. In short, the god of mammon promises to protect you from anything that would threaten your security or pleasure.

The Clash of the Gods

We are involved in a battle between the god of this world and the God of the universe. Both have made their proposals and both have benefits to offer. One of them offers instant pleasures that will be short-lived. The other offers short-term suffering but eternal, unspeakable joy. One requires only feeling—the other takes faith.

Choose You This Day

We have two options before us, and we must make a choice. Like the men at Athens who served many gods, we would like to believe we can bow down to the living God and the god of mammon and be blessed by both. Anticipating our tendency to have divided hearts, Jesus taught clearly that we cannot serve both God and mammon.

In a self-centered society drowning in materialism, the call today is for families to stand up, renounce the god of mammon, and commit every part of their lives, including their finances, to the Lord Jesus. The call is to radically proclaim, by their financial choices, that this world is not their home.

I want to begin this book with a word of hope. You may be deeply in debt because of poor decisions you made. You may have credit card debt, car loans, loans from parents, and a large home mortgage. This book is not intended to shame you for past mistakes. All of us have made many financial mistakes. All of us!

But be encouraged! There is a path of recovery from your present situation. It may not be painless or fun, but if you are serious about turning this area of your life over to the Lord, there is hope. Many Christians, after accumulating staggering amounts of debt, have been able to recover and live productive, debt-free lives with their finances free to bless others. May the Lord bless you as you recommit this area of your life to Him!

Part One
Practical Stewardship

CHAPTER ONE

The Influence of Affluence

Donald and Mary* stopped in one afternoon and said they wanted to talk a little about their finances. They had not been married long, but had already discovered that money can affect a marriage relationship. They were not overly concerned, just having a little difficulty with their cash flow. After some discussion I asked them to fill out a personal financial statement to get a picture of where they were. Their list of debts was lengthy. They had taken loans for two cars and had debts to parents, grandparents, local merchants, and various credit card companies. They had borrowed for trips, gifts, eating out, clothing, and various other items they had wanted along the way. For only being married a couple of years, they had done a remarkable job of acquiring debt.

Writing down their assets didn't take nearly as long. In fact, their total cash on hand, including savings, checking accounts, his wallet, and her purse, was less than fifty dollars. As they walked into my office that day, they carried two large drinks they had purchased from the local convenience store. I couldn't help mentally observing that the price of the drinks represented a good portion of their total net worth. But they didn't seem overly concerned.

They admitted things had been a little tight lately, which was why they had stopped in, but they were confident all would turn out fine. "In fact," they confided as they sipped their drinks, "we have committed our finances to the Lord, and we're confident He will see us through. After all, hasn't He promised to be with us to the end?" They spoke of

---

* Names and details have been changed throughout the book.

their desire that their new home would glorify God and took great comfort in verses like, "But my God shall supply all your need according to his riches in glory by Christ Jesus."[a]

Donald and Mary had both grown up in typical middle-class American families. They had grown up with plenty, including nice homes, nice vehicles, and vacations each year. Donald and Mary had assumed they would live their lives the same way. It was the only way of life they knew. They were not aware that their parents hadn't always lived at this level of affluence. They hadn't observed those early years when their parents struggled to balance their own budget. They hadn't seen the ways their parents had economized when first married.

There are many Donalds and Marys among us today. They have grown up in homes where everything was provided: abundant food, first-rate medical care, spacious homes, excellent clothing, and quality transportation. They have had every need, and most wants, fulfilled and now assume they will begin where their parents left off. They enter marriage with high expectations that include continuing at the same standard of living.

The Plus Couples

I think of these new families as the plus couples. They start out with a vision of owning a home, plus one or two late-model vehicles, plus eating

[a]Philippians 4:19

out occasionally, plus frequent little vacations, plus new home furnishings, plus name-brand clothing, plus the latest kitchen gadgetry, plus nice recreation equipment, plus cell phones for each spouse, plus . . .

Sociologists have referred to this generation as the "ME" generation. Society is teaching our families that life is all about them. They shouldn't have to wait for anything and they deserve the best. The focus is on instant gratification, the options seem infinite, and with easy credit, purchasing has never been easier.

Marketing Mania

Another powerful force is impacting the Donalds and Marys among us. Not only do they have great expectations and a sense of deserving the best, but they are also under intense marketing pressure. Their mailboxes are filled with advertisements each week, providing a virtual parade of enticing items through their homes. The colorful pictures show happy families gathered around the new couch, lawnmower, or stainless steel grill. The landscaping is professional, the well-dressed parents obviously love each other, and the children are playing nicely together. Even the dog is grinning.

All this joy, it is insinuated, is available when you purchase this new barbeque grill, which happens to be on sale this week for only $199. Is the budget a little tight this month? No problem. You can still have all this peace and happiness in your home for only $20 per month. And, if that isn't enough, you can take the grill home today and not pay anything for ninety days. Amazing! These people must really want to help you! How did they know you were a little short on cash this month?

Then, as if this constant bombardment from without were not enough, couples are also experiencing pressure from within. Peer pressure from within our close-knit church communities can be intense. As one couple gets the new grill, it applies pressure on others. After all, who wants to be the only couple who doesn't look prosperous? Of course, all of this wouldn't have much impact if barbeque grills were the only inessential items for sale. But today's markets are flooded with a seemingly endless array of unnecessary items and gadgets that tempt families.

How are couples to survive this constant onslaught? How can they save for a home when the cost of living is so high? Is it really possible for young families to survive on one income today with property being so expensive and energy, health, and transportation costs continuing to climb? Yet in spite of these odds, a healthy financial situation is possible. Many young families within our communities are not only flourishing, but are also using their money to bless those in need. How can they do it? How can they survive when it seems the current is against them?

The Influence of Affluence

Before answering these questions, perhaps we should look at where our young people have learned how to live. We have talked about the struggles facing our young families and the mindset many of them have regarding starting where their parents left off, but does all the blame for this mindset lie on the young? Sometimes those of us who are older tend to look at our young families and shake our heads. Why can't they live a little more simply? Why do they complain about the high cost of living while viewing items like cell phones, something we never had, as necessities?

We need to go back and look at the homes from which our children came. Is it possible that those of us who are older have neglected to teach by word and example in some of these areas? Have our children watched us voluntarily restrict our consumption in the midst of prosperity?

> **Have our children watched us voluntarily restrict our consumption in the midst of prosperity?**

Or could it be that our own love for the world has led some of our children down a wrong path? Perhaps we have forgotten the impact our level of consumption has on our children. Maybe we have ignored the powerful influence of affluence. Perhaps it is time we returned to basic foundational teaching concerning possessions, money, and stewardship. We need to return to the Bible.

Study Questions

1. Are young couples in your congregation struggling financially? If so, why?

2. How is the surrounding affluence affecting you?

3. Do you feel pressure from your social circle to live at a certain level?

4. Can you think of young couples who are good examples of simple living?

5. Are there older couples within your congregation who voluntarily restrict their consumption for the Kingdom? How does observing this affect your life?

Chapter Two
What Does the Bible Say?

The Bible is not silent on the topic of finance. The Old and New Testaments both contain a tremendous amount of teaching on the subject. There is teaching for those lending money as well as warning to the borrower. There is instruction for the man who is blessed with wealth and for the man who struggles financially and is tempted to covet. God gives direction on where, when, and how much to give. He explains both the result of seeking wealth and the consequences of idleness and slothfulness.

Money creates dilemmas for each of us. It would have been easier if God had said, "Just don't do money. Treat it like picking up sticks on the Sabbath—it's dangerous, so just leave it alone." That would be simpler, wouldn't it? Just treat it like you would stealing, lying, or murder. We know these things are out of God's will and we are to avoid them. But the Lord didn't do this with money. He warns us about it, tells us not to serve it, and even calls the love of it the root of all evil. Yet, after being told how dangerous this stuff is, we have to use it every day. Throughout our lifetime we carry something around in our pockets or purses that has the potential of destroying us! It is no wonder so much of the Bible's teaching is on money.

As we examine how a family is both to survive

> **Throughout our lifetime we carry something around in our pockets or purses that has the potential of destroying us!**

and properly use the financial resources God gives, it seems imperative that we begin by looking at what the Bible says. As we look at the professing Christianity that surrounds us, it becomes evident that there are varied interpretations of what the Bible means. This book is not an attempt to enter the debate of Biblical interpretation. Yet I am convinced the Lord has put the Bible together in a way which makes the essential things easy to understand and the less important more obscure. It is not His will that anyone be confused on issues that will be of utmost importance. God's Word contains relevant teachings that are not hard to understand or too difficult to live out. We will also find that living out these basic concepts is liberating, rather than confining.

When I was first asked to write this book, one of my concerns was that differences in understanding concerning issues of lesser importance not be allowed to obscure the significant. There have been many discussions, for example, on whether tithing is required in our day, or whether "Owe no man any thing" means that a man should never take out a loan. Some argue that the process of saving to purchase a home is laying up treasures on earth, and others disagree. Some fellowships have decided the word *usury* is speaking of interest regardless of the percentage, and others have determined that usury applies only to extremely high rates. These are important topics and should be discussed, but debating these interpretations is not the purpose of this book.

It is possible for Christians, after listening to endless debate, to dismiss the Bible as irrelevant, too vague, and not applicable for guidance in our day. If our young people conclude that the Bible is not relevant in our day in areas like finance, we have failed them. If a couple makes poor choices due to our endless debate on the trivial, we are partly to blame. The Bible is clear on some basic financial truths, and it is important that we do not get hung up on minor differences or issues.

Young people will also conclude the Bible is irrelevant if they fail to see older believers willing to take the teachings of Jesus seriously. It is important to stay as close as possible to the literal teaching of the Bible as we make financial decisions for our families. We want truth in every part of our lives regardless of the cost. We don't want to wait until after death to discover we were wrong.

It is important that we identify and understand some foundational Biblical truths before determining how smaller daily choices are to be made. I believe much of our current confusion in the areas of materialism and family finance stems from trying to build on an improper foundation. Let's take a look at some of these foundational Scriptural truths.

Everything Is the Lord's.

We all verbally affirm this truth, but many of our choices reveal our unbelief. In Psalm 50:12 the Lord says, "If I were hungry, I would not tell thee: for the world is mine, and the fulness thereof." This is a simple truth. Everything ultimately belongs to God. We are simply using and enjoying God's possessions. Everything around us—possessions, homes, lands, money—everything is the Lord's.

We should be able to understand this even in practical ways. We talk about paying off our homes as though once the mortgage is paid off, the house is really ours. But is it really? Just try not paying your taxes for a while and see who really owns it. But even the government is not the ultimate owner. Most land in the world has been passed around from regime to regime. Whoever is in power at the time controls it, but they do not really own it. Ultimately everything is God's. Everything that is currently in my name is just one heartbeat from being transferred to another.

> **Everything that is currently in my name is just one heartbeat from being transferred to another.**

While we all say this is true, our lives and attitudes reveal our struggle. We agree that the money in every man's pocket belongs to God, yet we seem preoccupied with whose pocket the money is currently in. But if everything belongs to the Lord, does it really matter if my brother comes out better in a business deal? A strong belief in this basic principle can be very freeing in our lives. When the house burns down, the bank fails, or someone breaks in and steals, a proper understanding of the real owner will have a dramatic effect on our reactions and anxiety levels.

We Are to Be Diligent.

The Bible is clear that God has placed His creation under our care and intends for us to be diligent in caring for it. This was God's vision from the beginning. Genesis 2:15 says, "And the Lord God took the man, and put him into the garden of Eden to dress it and to keep it." It was God's garden, as Adam soon found out, but it was Adam's responsibility to be diligent in caring for it. Many proverbs speak of God's desire for industry in our lives and the blessings of being diligent.

> Go to the ant, thou sluggard; consider her ways, and be wise: Which having no guide, overseer, or ruler, Provideth her meat in the summer, and gathereth her food in the harvest. How long wilt thou sleep, O sluggard? when wilt thou arise out of thy sleep? Yet a little sleep, a little slumber, a little folding of the hands to sleep: So shall thy poverty come as one that travelleth, and thy want as an armed man.[a]

God desires that we work diligently and with purpose. Even in the New Testament, where the focus is more on spiritual than natural wealth, Paul encouraged the brethren at Ephesus to be diligent. "Let him that stole steal no more: but rather let him labour, working with his hands the thing which is good, that he may have to give to him that needeth."[b]

Again in his first letter to the church at Thessalonica Paul wrote, ". . . and to do your own business, and to work with your own hands, as we commanded you."[c]

In his second letter he again reminded them of their need for diligence when he said, "For even when we were with you, this we commanded you, that if any would not work, neither should he eat."[d]

At times we try to separate the physical from the spiritual. We act as if God desires that we ignore the physical and focus solely on the spiritual. But is it okay to neglect balancing the checkbook because of our fervor for lost souls? No, God wants us to be diligent with what He has entrusted to our care, and a good portion of what He has given us to care for is part of the physical realm.

---

[a]Proverbs 6:6-11
[b]Ephesians 4:28
[c]1 Thessalonians 4:11
[d]2 Thessalonians 3:10

Debt Is Dangerous.

Listening to Biblical teaching regarding debt would aid us in avoiding many financial pitfalls. The Old Testament warns against it, and Jesus also used the illustration of debt in His parables. He told of individuals who were so far in debt there was no way they could repay. He talked about the relief that follows getting out of debt. Jesus used debt to teach about the relationship between being forgiven much and loving much. He also told of a man who had accumulated such a large debt that he was taken before the magistrates and threatened with prison. His wife and children were to be sold to fulfill his obligations. A secondary message in this parable is clear: debt is dangerous and must be repaid.

We would be wise to heed these lessons today. They didn't have Visa and MasterCard in Jesus' day. We don't read of ATMs just outside the temple, but debt was obviously as dangerous in their economy as it is in ours.

The writer of the Proverbs said it like this: "The rich ruleth over the poor, and the borrower is servant to the lender."ᵉ This is just as true in our modern economy as it was when written thousands of years ago. We like to think things are different now. We like to believe our economy is more stable and our income more secure. But the financial shakeup in recent years has revealed our economy to be unstable, and the borrower is still servant to the lender.

Many families today become convicted in the area of Biblical stewardship and would like to use more of their financial resources to bless the Kingdom. But they come face to face with a sad reality. Their poor financial decisions of the past keep them from sharing as they know they should. They are reminded of the truth of this Biblical principle each month as they write out checks to a myriad of financial institutions. The borrower is still servant to the lender. If we simply use the Bible instead of culture as our source of instruction, it will keep us from many snares. Debt is still dangerous.

Money Is an Indicator of the Heart.

Jesus said, "For where your treasure is, there will your heart be also."ᶠ Notice Jesus didn't say this was a possibility, or if we are not careful,

---

ᵉProverbs 22:7
ᶠMatthew 6:21

this will be the result. He said this is how it is. Our hearts follow our treasure. If you are really serious about discovering where your heart is before God, examine what you treasure.

But the opposite is also true. Our treasure tends to follow our hearts. Because of this, our use of money can be very useful in self-examination. We refer to money that is left after the necessities of life have been purchased as discretionary income. Analyzing what we do with our discretionary income can be a great revealer of our hearts.

If a man loves something, you can be sure his discretionary income will flow toward it. Consequently, if your money has a tendency to end up in antique or sporting goods stores, for example, you can be sure antiques or sporting goods hold a certain value in your heart. On the other hand, if your life has been transformed by the power of the Lord Jesus, you will find your money flowing toward needs He was concerned about while He lived here. You will find your treasure moving toward the downcast, the hurting, and the spiritually needy. Stop for a moment and consider. Where does your money go? After you have purchased everything needed for survival, what happens to the money that is left over?

Most of us are willing to admit there is danger in riches and a tendency for men who have wealth to trust in it. But somehow we like to think we are the exceptions. We like to believe it is possible to have earthly riches without wealth having an effect on our hearts. In fact, most believers in America today will tell you there is nothing wrong with piling up treasure in the bank as long as you keep it out of your heart. We like to think we are capable of having earthly treasure without it impacting our focus.

> **. . . somehow we like to think we are the exceptions.**

Psalm 62:10 says, "If riches increase, set not your heart upon them." The obvious inference here is that a man who has wealth will tend to put his trust in his money. In a time of ease and affluence we need to go back and look at this basic truth again. Our checkbooks can be good indicators of where our hearts are. Or perhaps we could say our hearts are wherever our treasure has been going. Take a moment and analyze this truth in your own life. Where has your money been going?

Earthly Wealth Is Not Trustworthy.

The writer of Proverbs said, "Riches certainly make themselves wings; they fly away as an eagle toward heaven."[g] Earthly wealth is simply not reliable. Jesus emphasized this truth in the Sermon on the Mount when He said, "Lay not up for yourselves treasures upon earth, where moth and rust doth corrupt, and where thieves break through and steal."[h]

Jesus was giving sound financial advice. Notice He did not tell us to refrain from investing; rather, He was doing what good financial advisers have always done. Financial advisers are hired to tell us where our money will be safe and where we can receive the best return on our investments.

This is what Jesus did. He wants us to invest, but He wants us to invest where our money will be safe and provide the best return. In fact, Jesus was so excited about the return on investment that He even advised people to sell their possessions to enable them to invest more. "Sell that ye have, and give alms; provide yourselves bags which wax not old, a treasure in the heavens that faileth not, where no thief approacheth, neither moth corrupteth."[i]

No financial adviser would give this kind of advice unless he was very sure about the investment he was encouraging. There was a reason Jesus could be confident in giving financial advice: He knew the future. He knew that everything we see around us will soon be worthless. True value can be found in the eternal alone.

Wealth Can Deceive and Destroy.

Jesus was very clear. Wealth is dangerous. He spent an amazing amount of time warning on the deceitfulness of riches. If Jesus had given as much warning against Coca-Cola as he did the pursuit of earthly wealth, we would never touch the stuff! As we read the words of Jesus on this topic, each of us should ask, "Am I as alarmed about the effect of wealth on my life as Jesus was?" Before answering this question, let's look at the familiar account in the New Testament of Jesus' encounter with the rich young ruler. Take the time to read this account again and then examine your own heart.

---

[g]Proverbs 23:5
[h]Matthew 6:19
[i]Luke 12:33

And when he was gone forth into the way, there came one running, and kneeled to him, and asked him, Good Master, what shall I do that I may inherit eternal life? And Jesus said unto him, Why callest thou me good? there is none good but one, that is, God. Thou knowest the commandments, Do not commit adultery, Do not kill, Do not steal, Do not bear false witness, Defraud not, Honour thy father and mother. And he answered and said unto him, Master, all these have I observed from my youth. Then Jesus beholding him loved him, and said unto him, One thing thou lackest: go thy way, sell whatsoever thou hast, and give to the poor, and thou shalt have treasure in heaven: and come, take up the cross, and follow me. And he was sad at that saying, and went away grieved: for he had great possessions. And Jesus looked round about, and saith unto his disciples, How hardly shall they that have riches enter into the kingdom of God! And the disciples were astonished at his words. But Jesus answereth again, and saith unto them, Children, how hard is it for them that trust in riches to enter into the kingdom of God! It is easier for a camel to go through the eye of a needle, than for a rich man to enter into the kingdom of God. And they were astonished out of measure, saying among themselves, Who then can be saved?[j]

This passage of Scripture has been analyzed, scrutinized, and rationalized since the days of the early Christians. We do word studies, go back to the Greek, and give many differing explanations. Some say Jesus could see this rich ruler's heart, and the teaching to sell all he had was intended only for this ruler in his particular situation. Others have said that the teaching of giving away all possessions is for all believers of all ages. They point to Luke 12:33, where Jesus gave almost the same command to his disciples, as proof that Jesus intended this instruction for all His followers. Some have said that we just don't understand the language, culture, and setting. Jesus wasn't talking about

[j]Mark 10:17-26

a literal camel and needle at all, and those words were just figurative language telling us not to trust in wealth. It is acceptable to have riches—just don't trust in them.

But as I have listened to this ongoing discussion, one thing has perplexed me. I haven't observed much difference in the lifestyles of those who interpret this Scripture in drastically different ways. One brother who lives in a congregation where they have chosen to have no savings told me recently he doesn't believe their congregation is giving any more than the churches around them. Instead of having savings accounts, they tend to put more money into their businesses.

Another brother from a congregation where they allow savings accounts but refuse to receive interest on their money confided that many of their wealthier members have put their money into rental property. If you can't get any income off money in savings, why not put it somewhere you can? Somehow we find ways to get around well-intended guidelines.

There is nothing wrong with setting up guidelines to guard against our materialistic culture. I believe some collective guidelines could help more of our Anabaptist communities in the area of materialism, and I appreciate leadership in the area of stewardship. But perhaps the answer is not perfect guidelines or a correct interpretation of this passage regarding the rich young ruler. Maybe we have simply failed to continually remind ourselves of the effect of wealth on our hearts. Perhaps we have failed to exhort each other daily. Maybe we haven't been as diligent as they were in the time of Malachi where it says, "Then they that feared the Lord spake often one to another."[k]

We have underestimated the impact of wealth upon our spiritual lives, and regardless of our interpretation of the account of the rich young ruler, I think it is foolish to ignore the disciples' response. This is something we can all understand. Mark says when Jesus had finished talking to the rich young ruler and had explained the connection between wealth and salvation, the disciples were "astonished out of measure, saying among themselves, Who then can be saved?" In other words, whatever it was that Jesus meant shocked the disciples to the core.

[k]Malachi 3:16

Now honestly examine your own view of wealth and finances. If you were to explain to your neighbors how you view wealth and finances, how would it affect them? If you were to explain your beliefs about possessions, borrowing, saving, and riches in general, how would they respond? Would it shock them? Would they be astonished beyond measure? Or would they say, "That is a little different than we view it, but it doesn't sound unreasonable."

Let's go back to our original question. "Am I as alarmed about the effect of wealth on my life as Jesus was?" Each of us should take this question before the Lord in prayer. We live in a society that values money and possessions very highly, and being surrounded by this false value system has a tremendous effect on us.

In Jesus' lesson regarding the sower who went forth to sow, He said that the man who "received seed among the thorns is he that heareth the word; and the care of this world, and the deceitfulness of riches, choke the word, and he becometh unfruitful."[l]

I believe those of us living in America today have received the Word among thorns. We have grown up in an environment of materialism where faith in God is difficult to maintain. We have greatly underestimated the effect wealth can have on our spiritual lives. We are in danger of being so in love with wealth and the enjoyment it brings that we succumb to the temptation of circumventing Scripture. As Ron Sider said in his book *Rich Christians in an Age of Hunger,* "We insist on more and more, and reason that if Jesus was so un-American that He considered riches dangerous, then we must ignore or re-invent His message."[1]

Those are serious words we would do well to consider. We live in a time of great deception, a time when the Bible says men will be "lovers of pleasures more than lovers of God."[m] We need to actively warn, encourage, and exhort each other daily regarding the danger of our surroundings and culture, and so much more as we see the day approaching.

We Are to Be Content.

When John the Baptist first began his ministry, one of his first instructions to those who would enter this new Kingdom was that they

---

[l]Matthew 13:22
[m]2 Timothy 3:4

should be content with their wages. Contentment has been an issue since the Fall in the garden, but I believe we are seeing an exponential increase in discontentment in modern times. Why is this?

Take a walk back through the past sixty years. The average American's life has changed tremendously since 1950. Sixty years ago, eating at a restaurant was a delight and something to remember. Just the thought of eating in town brought a thrill to the heart of a child. Today, in many of our homes, one or more of the members eat in town frequently, if not on a regular basis. The thrill is gone.

Sixty years ago people waited to purchase certain types of fruit until they were in season. The first ripe strawberries brought excitement. Today many are not even aware that fruits have seasons. We push shopping carts past fresh food flown in from all around the world, and woe to the grocery store that doesn't keep up. Many children in America have lost the excitement of that first strawberry. They consume them in January without a thought. Again, the thrill is gone.

Consider housing. Following World War II, the average size of an American home was around 750 square feet. During the fifties the average climbed to 950 square feet, and in the sixties the average rose to about 1,100. If you grew up in a 750-square-foot home and finally were able to afford a 1,100-square-foot home, you were thrilled. After all, your new home was almost 50 percent larger than the old.

During the seventies, new homes were up to an average of 1,350 square feet, and now the average home being built is over 2,300 square feet.[2] And all this happened during a time when average family size was shrinking. Today it is not uncommon to find two people living in a 5,000-square-foot house. The average American feels constricted in his 2,300-square-foot home. The closets are full, the car is in the driveway because the garage is full, and meanwhile the bills keep coming from the mini-storage facility in town. Our homes are bigger than ever, but the thrill is gone.

How did we get here? Why do we have so much, yet continually long for even more? While these questions may have many answers, I am convinced much of our difficulty is a result of using an improper point of reference. We tend to base our expectations on what we observe in our peers and neighbors. The Bible tells us not to compare ourselves among ourselves, yet we do. We notice how often our neighbors eat out, how large their homes are, and how often they take vacations, and it subtly affects our choices. We watch what types of vehicles they purchase and how many bells and whistles they have.

But what would our lives look like if we used the Bible to establish our expectations and make our choices? What if we really used Biblical truth as our point of reference? How many of our financial struggles are simply a result of using somebody or something other than the Word of God as our standard? And perhaps more important, how many of our resources could be used for the Kingdom, assisting people around the world who have real needs?

We often shy away from addressing this topic. We are afraid to exhort our brother, knowing that our own lives are inconsistent. Ministers are slow to speak plainly on this topic due to fear of being examined personally. But thankfully the Apostle Paul was not afraid to address the need for contentment. In his letter to Timothy he said, "But godliness with contentment is great gain. For we brought nothing into this world, and it is certain we can carry nothing out. And having food and raiment let us be therewith content."[n]

This verse may be 2,000 years old, but I wonder if it has ever been more applicable than today. Food and raiment. Could you be content with that? Enough to eat and protection against the elements—is that enough? Or do you find, as you look into your heart, that your list has gradually grown, influenced by the culture that surrounds you?

We Are to Seek God First.

Jesus told the people that day on the mountainside, "But seek ye first the kingdom of God, and his righteousness; and all these things shall be added unto you."[o] Is that really a promise? Does God really care about our physical well-being?

I remember hearing a minister in a Third World country tell a story to illustrate God's faithfulness. He had many children and lived in a large city, and within the last month his family had experienced a

---

[n]1 Timothy 6:6-8
[o]Matthew 6:33

crisis. They were completely out of food and he was out of work, so he gathered the family around him that evening, and they spent quite a while pouring out their need to their heavenly Father. Night came, and they still did not have any food. So they decided to get up early the next day to again seek God's blessing. After praying for a while the next morning, they all went out to see if they could find work or food.

That evening they gathered again. None of them had been successful, so again they prayed and went to bed with empty stomachs. The next morning they got up early to pray, and this time they decided to continue praying until later in the morning. They prayed until around eleven o'clock, when a neighbor knocked on the door, interrupting their prayer. The neighbor stood at the door with some milk to share, and it was enough for each of them to have some.

Listening to this story, I was overcome by a level of poverty I knew nothing of and persistence in prayer that challenged me. But neither

of these issues was the focus of this young minister. He was telling the story to illustrate God's faithfulness, showing that God will reward us if we seek Him. He just couldn't stop talking about how wonderfully God had provided.

Is that what you got out of this story? Was that the feature of this account that impressed you? Or did it seem to you God could have responded a little sooner and provided something a little more substantial than milk from a neighbor?

Do you really believe that God cares about your physical needs? This young minister was looking to God for His needs, not his wants. In spite of doctrines floating around in "Christianity" today, God has not promised us a three-bedroom, two-bath home with an SUV in the driveway. But He has promised to provide what we really need if we seek Him first.

Examine your own life. What are you primarily seeking? Are you pursuing "God and His righteousness" first, or "all these things"? I have never been in a situation like this young minister's. I have never known real hunger. I have experienced plenty all my life, and I tend to get my wants and needs confused. While God's list of "all these things" may be some milk after hours of prayer, my list tends to be much longer; and if I am not careful, it continues to grow.

Conclusion

These are just a few of the basic Scriptural truths regarding finance. Many other important teachings could be considered, and the Bible is full of practical advice on how our money is to be regarded and used. You may be asking, "What do all these Biblical teachings have to do with my current financial problems? How will a few Biblical teachings help the fact that my credit cards are maxed and there is never quite enough in the checkbook?" The reason we are starting with the basics is very simple and very important. Before we consider how to get out of debt, I believe it is essential to examine why we are in debt to start with.

Most of our struggles in the area of personal finance come because we attempt to build on an improper foundation. We try to divorce Biblical truth from practical living. But if you can embrace these basic truths, they will have a tremendous impact on your life and finances. I marvel at how applicable Biblical financial principles, written thousands of years ago, are today.

At times I have difficulty understanding some of our Lord's teachings on finance. But I wonder if the teachings are actually unclear or if I simply do not have an open heart to obey. We need to hold our hearts up before the Lord constantly in prayer. We need continual self-examination. Do I really want truth? If it is God's desire that I give more, or that I use less of His resources on myself, do I really want to know this? These are soul-searching questions.

I want to encourage families to take the area of finance before the Lord in prayer. Spend time together in the Bible looking at what God has to say. The Bible contains many family devotions on this topic, and I am confident that as you seek God, He will provide direction, your marriage relationship will be strengthened, and your children will grow up understanding that the Bible is our most valuable resource for practical living.

Study Questions

1. How will believing that everything belongs to the Lord affect your life?

2. Is it possible to give finances too little or too much consideration? How would you know if you are doing this?

3. How can debt affect our decisions? How can it affect how we read the teachings of Jesus?

4. How can our use of money reveal our hearts?

5. If you would describe your views on money and possessions to your neighbors, how would they respond? Would your views seem strange to them? As they watch how you live, are they puzzled?

6. Do your neighbors view you as a contented individual?

CHAPTER THREE
Steward or Owner?

In the Old Testament God often rewarded men materially for their faithfulness to Him. Deuteronomy has an abundance of physical promises for the man who follows God faithfully. Abraham, Job, David, and Solomon are examples of men whom God rewarded materially for their faithfulness.

But in the Kingdom of Jesus Christ it is obviously different. Jesus clearly warned His disciples that a decision to follow Him would mean adversity in this life. Choosing to follow Christ may mean losing land, houses, and friends. We may be asked to choose between God and earthly possessions. History is full of men who have literally done this. They have voluntarily liquidated their possessions and given them to the poor upon deciding to follow the Lord Jesus.

When we choose to follow Jesus, we take nothing with us. Our old life of ownership is over and Jesus now owns all. Paul, in his letter to the church at Corinth, reminded them they are now simply the temple of

> **When we choose to follow Jesus, we take nothing with us. Our old life of ownership is over and Jesus now owns all.**

God. He is to have total control. Don't you understand that "ye are not your own?" he asked them. "For ye are bought with a price: therefore glorify God in your body, and in your spirit, which are God's."[a]

This truth should have a powerful impact on our finances. This means

---

[a]1 Corinthians 6:19-20

that the cash in our wallets, the money in our checking accounts, and the properties with our names on the deeds are not ours but God's.

So, now that we are stewards instead of owners, just what is the role of a steward?

The Role of a Steward

Sometimes I hear my wife ask one of our daughters to stop by the grocery store to purchase a few items while she is in town. She will normally give our daughter a list of items needed and some money. When our daughter is given the money, I have observed that she usually does not put it in with her own personal money. She may be carrying a purse, but the money from Mother is usually placed in a sweater pocket or some separate place so it doesn't get mixed with her personal cash. Why is this?

The money is kept separate because our daughter understands it is not really hers, even though she is carrying it. It was given to her for a particular purpose and is not to be used for anything else. It still belongs to Mother. As she drives out the lane and heads for town, Mother is the owner and she is simply the steward.

When our daughter returns and delivers the items, my wife thanks her and then asks, "Where is the change?" More money was sent along with our daughter than was needed for the purchase, and my wife expects to receive the extra money.

Now let's suppose my wife sent a twenty-dollar bill along, and all she needed from town was one loaf of bread and a gallon of milk. Let's assume the total cost of these items was five dollars. She would expect fifteen back, wouldn't she? Now let's imagine the following scenario when our daughter returned home:

"Thank you for buying these items. Do you have the change for me?"

"Here it is, Mother."

"Only two dollars? How much did the milk and bread cost?"

"Five dollars."

"Well, I gave you twenty dollars. What happened to the other thirteen?"

"Oh, I forgot to mention that. I was driving past Starbucks, and they have this new caramel frappuccino blended coffee drink. It has chopped ice, different coffees, and milk blended in, and a whipped cream topping. Wow, it was so good! And while I was there, I just couldn't resist trying a couple of those cranberry scones. They were kind of expensive, but they tasted so good!"

Now how do you think Mother would respond? I don't know how a conversation like this would end in your home, but I know that in ours, Mother wouldn't be very happy. She had trusted her daughter to be a steward of her money, and her daughter had failed. If she'd had a flat tire or needed to purchase fuel, which pertained to the mission, Mother would have understood. But a drink at Starbucks hardly qualified. At some point, money consumed by a steward for personal gratification becomes theft.

Now consider this illustration as it applies to your life. God has entrusted a portion of His resources into your care. Some of His resources may be in your bank account or in your possessions. God intends for His stewards to use part of these resources to survive. Each of us needs to eat, have shelter, and purchase clothing. God understands this. But after these needs are met, what happens to the balance of the resources in your care?

Where's the Change?

We should be sobered by the reality of meeting our God someday. As He reviews the abundant resources He has entrusted into our care, He might have a question for us. Perhaps, as in the scenario above, He will ask, "Where is the change?"

An owner has a perfect right to spend his money however he wishes. After all, it is his money! But a steward oversees goods that are not his own. If we can allow the Lord to implant this basic truth in our hearts, it will have a transforming effect on our finances. Stewardship is not just a nice concept; it is a reality in the lives of many Kingdom believers who are serious about their walk with the Lord Jesus.

Many of our financial difficulties come from neglecting the principle of stewardship. Instead of focusing on the Word of God, we focus on the materialistic society we live in. Its goals become our goals.

Its expectations become ours, and we forget our reason for being here on earth. We take our eyes off the reality that God has purchased us through the blood of the Lord Jesus and we are not our own. All the things we once called our own have been surrendered to Him, and this includes our finances. Although the bank account has my name on it, I am simply a steward of my Lord's goods.

Let's consider one more example. Most of us are familiar with delivery trucks. A United Parcel Service truck probably stops at all our homes at least occasionally. We look forward to his visits and usually wonder what the UPS man is bringing today. But as we consider Christian stewardship, let's think about the role of the UPS man. The goods he brings do not belong to him, but are temporarily under his care. He is a steward of the goods he carries.

Is it difficult for the UPS man to take a package worth hundreds of dollars from his truck and leave it on your step? Keep in mind, he is delivering things that may be worth more than his wages for the whole week or even the month. Does this bother him? Of course not. The delivery man understands this is his job. In fact, he probably wouldn't keep his job long if he started taking some of the valuable goods home with him and using them for his own gratification.

God's Delivery Men

As stewards, we are God's delivery men. God gives us resources, intending for us to deliver them. Paul, in writing to the church at Ephesus and speaking of the believer, said, "Let him labour, working with his hands . . . that he may have to give to him that needeth."[b]

The next time you see a UPS driver, remember you are in possession of God's resources, and as a believer, you are God's delivery man.

In a capitalistic society we begin regarding resources as something we have earned that therefore belongs to us. We begin to equate financial success with good choices. If the things I have are a result of good choices, we tell ourselves, then I have earned them and they belong to me. If they belong to me, then they are for my own pleasure and enjoyment. But Jesus has called us to surrender our earthly possessions.

> **. . . as a believer, you are God's delivery man.**

In his book *Money, Possessions, and Eternity*, Randy Alcorn says it this way:

> When we come to grasp that we are stewards, not owners of our money, it totally changes our perspective. Suddenly I'm not asking, "How much of my money shall I, out of the goodness of my heart, give to God?" Rather, I'm asking, "Since all of 'my' money is really yours, Lord, how would you like me to invest your money today?"[3]

Being a faithful steward is more than just abstaining from extravagant homes, expensive vacations, costly recreational equipment, or luxury vehicles. It is recognizing that all we have is God's and that we must put God's resources to work. Being a faithful steward means investing God's resources where God would want them invested.

Should I Just Not Spend?

Sometimes we speak with disdain about those who spend huge amounts on extravagant lifestyles. "What a waste!" we exclaim. "Why couldn't all this money have been used to help those who are starv-

---

[b]Ephesians 4:28

ing?" We raise our eyebrows at those who have private jets or several homes. Something is wrong in a world where a few have so much and most have so little. Even the early Christians recognized how ugly overindulgence is. One of the early writers said it like this: "To live in luxury is a sin, for it is monstrous for one to live in luxury, while many are in want."[4]

But before we come down too hard on the extremely rich, perhaps we should look within. Spending vast amounts of money on ourselves, as Clement said, is certainly sin, but are we innocent of wasting our Lord's goods in other ways? How does our Father view idle money sitting in the bank while many of His children are in need? Looking at "our" resources through the lens of Biblical stewardship will affect every part of our financial decision making.

The Best Investment

When Jesus told the rich young ruler to sell all he had and give to the poor, I think that is all the rich man heard. His focus was on what he would lose. But Jesus didn't just tell him to give up something; He was trying to sell the best investment this world has ever known. This man was so focused on earthly treasure that he missed the potential of the heavenly. I am sure this ruler had trained his eye to look for a good return on investments. He knew how to spot value and security. Investments are a balance between risk and return, and he knew how to identify a good deal. But he missed the best one. Jesus was offering an investment opportunity that has no equal: absolute security and eternal returns.

Conclusion

As we conclude our brief consideration of Biblical stewardship, it is important to remember that money is not our only resource. God has given each of us personal talents, relationships with people, and even our intellect and education.

Consider for a moment your stewardship and use of time. Do you view your time as your own to be used for your pleasure, or have you joyfully given this part of your life to the Lord? When we surrender our lives to the Lord Jesus, we are pledging to use every resource within our control for His Kingdom. This will have a profound effect on our recreational time and pursuits. Now our purpose for living is to promote and advance the Lord's Kingdom! We have no personal agendas. Our lives have been crucified and we are living for Him alone.

But sometimes we need to stop in self-examination. Is this a reality in our lives? Analyze your own heart. It is easy to say that we are followers of Jesus Christ. We enjoy singing songs like "Jesus, I my cross have taken, all to leave and follow thee." Nice words, but sometimes our choices in life tell a different story. As we continue to seek the face of God, He is faithful in bringing areas to mind where we lack total surrender. His goal is to gradually and graciously conform us to the image of Jesus. Let the Lord speak to your heart as you consider this question: Do my choices in life reflect that I am a steward or an owner?

Perhaps you have trouble relating to having extra time and unneeded money sitting in a bank. Maybe all of your time and money is spent trying to stay ahead of monthly payments from past purchases. If this is your situation, it is important to learn from the past as you plan for the future. Ask yourself this simple question: How much less would I be paying per month if I would have simply embraced a proper view of stewardship in the past?

Study Questions

1. When someone takes or damages "your" possessions, do you tend to respond as a steward or an owner?

2. How often do you consider standing before God and giving an account of your use of money?

3. How do you think God views idle money sitting in the bank while many are in need? Does God view this differently from making selfish purchases?

4. What aspect of Jesus' offer did the rich young ruler neglect to consider? Do you ever forget to consider the potential return on investment when money is used for the Kingdom?

5. Do you tend to think of "spare time" as belonging to you for your pleasure? How do you use a Saturday when nothing is on the schedule?

CHAPTER FOUR
Pursuing God's Vision for Our Finances

W e live about two hours from the nearest major airport. I have driven there enough to know about how long it takes to cross the mountain pass, drive through the traffic, park at an off-site parking lot, and ride the shuttle to the airport. Typically I look at the flight time on my ticket and then figure backward so I know what time I should leave home. Deciding on a time to leave is important, but it is the first of many decisions that must be made if I am to arrive at the airport on time.

Many plans in life are like this. We first establish an overriding goal. In the case above, it is to arrive at the airport at a certain time. We can refer to this as our master plan. Then we begin making smaller choices that line up with our overriding goal. Let's take a look at the scenario above to see how this works.

My plan is to arrive at the airport in two hours. We will call this my overriding goal. With this in mind, I load my luggage and drive out the lane. When I get to the end of my driveway, I am faced with a simple choice. I can turn right or left. Although this choice is simple, it is very important. Turning the wrong way will ultimately affect whether or not I catch my flight.

My drive to the airport is filled with little decisions like this one. Enticing options come along as I drive, and as each opportunity comes, I must make a choice. I pass numerous exits, shopping centers, a ski resort, places that advertise excellent food, and several sightseeing spots. But these attractions along the way provide little temptation. The advertisements are enticing, and I have been waylaid by the occasional

Krispy Kreme doughnut, but for the most part, I am oblivious to the options along the road.

There is a simple reason for this: none of these attractions line up with my overriding goal. I know I cannot stop at these places and still be at the airport on time. The vision I must keep before my eyes is my arrival time. It is not that I do not enjoy any of the things designed to distract me along the way. What keeps me on the road is the simple fact that none of the choices beside the road are as important to me as arriving at the airport on time.

Following a financial vision for your home is similar to my drive to the airport. If you are to be successful in reaching your financial goals, whatever they are, you must make each small decision along the way in light of your overriding vision.

Where Are We?

When starting out on a journey, you must first establish where you are. A map is worthless if you don't know your current position. You may know where you want to go and be able to identify it on the map, but it is impossible to chart a course to that location if you don't know where you are. Once you establish your present location, you have a reference point. The same is true when charting a financial course. It is important to take a close look at where you are right now.

Where Do We Want to Go?

The next thing that must be planned before venturing off is where we want to go. This point, like the first, is absolutely essential. Just imagine a husband and wife getting into a car and heading down the road without considering their ultimate destination. They drive down the road, merrily making each choice based on what feels right at the time. Occasionally they look at the fuel gauge and smile. They are not going to let an almost empty tank ruin their trip; after all, the engine is still running and they are keeping up with all the other cars.

As you watch them travel, it becomes obvious that they are making some of their decisions solely on the basis of what others are doing. If they notice the majority of cars going in a different direction, they happily turn and travel that direction for a while. If they see bright lights and signs offering something enticing in another direction, the steering wheel turns again. It does not take much intelligence to comprehend that this method of travel is a delightful way to end up far from where

you want to be. The result of traveling with no destination in mind is that a person will likely end up out of gas and far from home.

But as foolish as this means of navigation may appear, it is a good illustration of how many people operate their personal finances. Day after day goes by, and decisions are based on what seems good at the time. Paychecks come in, money goes out, and choices are made simply because something felt right at that moment. All options are viewed in light of the short term, and little thought is given to where each of these choices will take them. Sometimes decisions are made simply because of peer pressure, and other times a good sales pitch on the heels of a paycheck will make them change course.

Later on we will discuss how to determine long-term goals, but for now I simply want to point out the importance of having them. It is important for each family to establish its own financial goals. What is important to you as a family? Even more significant, what is important to God? Since you have committed your family to God and desire to follow a path of Biblical stewardship, you will want to use all the resources He has placed in your care as He would have you use them. It is important to give thought and prayer to where you want to go.

How Can We Get There?

It has been said, "If you don't care where you are going, then any old road will work." But the opposite is also true. If you have a desired destination, choosing a road is very important. Once you know where you are and have established where you want to go, you will want to find the best road.

We normally use a map to do this on a road trip. We might circle where we are and the place we want to go, then we look for the best roads to take us from one point to the other. Typically we look for the shortest path between these points, but not always. Sometimes going around a city on a bypass is a longer path, but because of traffic, it takes less time. There are other things to consider. If we want to arrive as quickly as possible, then we may look for interstates or highways where the speed limits are higher. If we prefer the scenic route, we may choose the back roads.

Just as we would use a map for a road trip, we use a budget to determine how to travel from our present location to our financial destination. Typically we do not have just one goal in mind, and consideration must be given to how goals can be balanced. For example, one of your goals may be to save for a home. But all your paycheck cannot go toward saving for a house. Your car is also accruing many miles and will probably need to be replaced within a few years. Most of us have more than one financial goal, and this can become a difficult balancing act. But this is also where a good budget can be beneficial. It becomes the road map that shows us the path between where we are and where we want to go.

Staying on Course

We have briefly discussed the importance of knowing where we are, deciding where we want to go, and mapping out a course between the two. But one of the universal struggles in personal finances is simply staying on the path we have charted out. Most of us have tried to set financial goals in the past—perhaps to give more or to pay off debt. But most of us have experienced failure because we didn't stay on the course we mapped out. Sometimes this is due to an emergency, but many times it is simply that we didn't keep our eyes on the goal. We made seemingly insignificant decisions and purchases that were not in line with our overriding vision, and we lost our way.

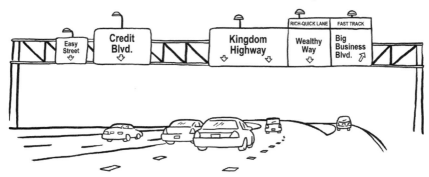

Benjamin Franklin once said, "Beware of little expenses. A small leak will sink a great ship." This basic truth is still as true today as it was in colonial America. Later we want to look in greater detail at this common tendency and at steps we can take to keep our personal finances on course.

Conclusion

Perhaps all this seems complicated, time-consuming, and unnecessary. Maybe what you would like is for someone to give you three easy steps to rescue you from your current financial situation. It is possible that is all your situation requires, but if so, your situation is rare. Many young families have difficulty with their finances because they are constantly looking for an easy, short-term solution. It can be a tremendous blessing to a home when a family takes time to analyze where they are financially, decide where they want to go, and plan how to get there. In the next chapters we'll take a closer look at these points and find practical ways to apply them.

I was recently talking to a young woman who grew up in a poor country. Her father has never made much money, yet he is known locally as a good manager. His children also exhibit good financial judgment, so I asked her how her father taught them. She said one of her favorite memories is of Saturday night discussions. After evening devotions her father would talk a little about the coming week and some of the financial needs they had. Sometimes it was a food supply they were low on, or maybe an item they needed but didn't have funds for. Each of them would suggest ways they could help reach this goal in the next week. Sometimes it meant doing without something, but she looks back on those family talks with joy. She felt like she was a part of the family and part of the solution, and though they had little money, she didn't feel poor.

Her father was doing what we have just discussed. He was assessing the current situation and then allowing his family to be actively involved in attaining their goal. But he was doing more than just reaching a weekly goal. He was also teaching his children how to survive and live responsibly when they had families of their own.

Study Questions

1. Which do you find more difficult, deciding on a vision and purpose for your life or making little choices consistent with this vision?

2. Give an example of a time you made a financial decision simply because of what others were doing.

3. Why is it important to have long-term goals for your finances? What could be the result of neglecting this?

4. Give an example of a time when you made a financial goal, but then neglected staying with it. What caused you to drift from your original vision?

5. Share some ways families can encourage each other to stay on track. What kind of topics could be used in family devotions?

Part Two
Where Are We?

CHAPTER FIVE

Finding Out Where We Are

They had been having some financial difficulties, but I really had no idea how bad their situation was. As I met George and Sally in their home that evening, I was expecting a short, enjoyable discussion. I hoped to share a few basic pointers and a little encouragement before going back home to my own family. They were both cheerful as I met them at the door.

As we sat around the kitchen table and began to discuss their situation, George admitted he had made a few mistakes along the way, and Sally took responsibility for their current situation as well. But as I tried to gather information so we could start working toward a solution, I began to notice something. Neither George nor Sally could give me definite answers regarding their finances. They were in trouble, but the only reason they knew it was because creditors had been calling them on a regular basis, and there was never quite enough money in the checking account to pay everyone.

Finally, after much fruitless questioning, I took a blank piece of paper and told George and Sally to write down all the debts they had at that time. Well, they knew they had a mortgage on their home, so Sally went to the next room and soon returned with the last statement on their loan. George mentioned a couple of credit cards with balances on them, but he couldn't remember just how many cards they had. He went into the adjoining room and returned with some information. Sally remembered another piece of mail she had seen, so she went back to the adjoining room and returned with more statements from additional credit card companies.

They continued these trips into the adjoining room, and I began to write down the various loan balances on my sheet of paper. With each newly discovered statement, my hope for a brief meeting dwindled. This wasn't looking very promising. But suddenly something occurred to me. Almost all these statements were coming out of envelopes that had not been opened before I arrived. Getting up from the table, I walked into the room where George and Sally were looking for more statements, and what I saw confirmed my fears. Sitting in a corner was a large grocery bag of unopened statements. As George and Sally continued digging through the bag, it became obvious why they didn't know how far in debt they were. They had stopped opening their mail.

They had charged on cards until each account had reached its limit, but since more cards kept coming in the mail, there had always been a card for the present need. George and Sally were glibly cheerful through this process because they were ignoring their actual situation. They had not been concerned about the state of their finances until they realized that their income was insufficient to make all their minimum payments.

Your situation may not be like George and Sally's, but many of us share a similar trait. George and Sally stopped opening their mail because it was too depressing. It became too discouraging to look at all those numbers again, so they didn't. Consequently they had no idea how bad their situation was. But failing to look at a problem seldom fixes it.

Don't Confuse Me With Facts

Many of us do the same thing on a different scale. We may not have a heavy debt load like George and Sally, but we dread sitting down and looking at all those numbers again. It just seems discouraging. As husbands, we bring home what seems like a large paycheck only to discover it isn't quite enough. Our checkbook seems somewhat like a kitchen sieve. The money disappears as fast as we pour it in.

Sometimes the wife takes care of the finances, and as husbands, it is easy to find ourselves frustrated. Why can't she do a better job of managing? How can one family go through so much money? Many times a wife would like to sit down and show her husband where the money is going, but the process is too painful and the husband avoids it. He would rather nurse frustration than get facts. Budgeting takes too much time, and after going out and working all day to make money, the last thing he feels like doing is sitting down and discussing it. He would rather just put the paycheck in the bank, write out checks for the things they need, and then see if there is money left over for the things they want.

In some families the husband oversees the finances. He tries to control how much money is going out, and since he isn't the one making the difficult decisions in the store, he can't understand why expenses are so high each month. In this case the wife may be the one who avoids sitting down to talk about the budget, since she always feels condemned in the end. No matter how frugal she thinks she is, it is never enough. And so the wife tends to avoid discussing finances. She just wants enough in the account to purchase what she needs. This communication problem plays out in various ways in every home, but it is a rare home that avoids the struggle entirely. It has been said that disagreement over money is the number one reason for divorce.

As we discussed earlier, it is of utmost importance that a husband and wife discuss and be fully aware of the state of their finances, regardless of who is in charge of the checkbook. It is important that either the husband or wife take primary responsibility for overseeing the finances, and it is essential that good communication occur between the two.

Many of us have no real sense of where we are financially. We only know that there is more month than money. Finding ourselves in this situation should inspire us to look for solutions, but often we find it easier to procrastinate. We rest in the illusion that next month things will miraculously improve, and we hope there will either be less month or more money.

How Can We Find Out Where We Are?

We have discussed the importance of finding out where we are, but how do we actually do this? Over time, our finances tend to become a jumble. We have mortgages, car payments, private loans from family members, checking and savings accounts, and credit cards. How can we really understand where we are as we begin to plot a course toward our goals? Let's briefly look at some ways we can identify where we are.

- Create a basic financial statement, including a list of debts. Taking the time to fill out a basic financial statement is extremely important. If you have outstanding debts, you will need to list the current balance for each of the loans as well as the interest rate on that loan and the monthly payment. We will discuss this in more detail later.

- Track spending history. This may take some time, depending on your past record keeping, but the intent is to find out where your money has been going. The farther back you can go, the better, but you should have at least three months of spending to look at.

- After tracking your spending, compare your present spending within each category to an average or healthy budget. This will tell you if you are spending too much on groceries, transportation, or recreation, based on your total monthly income. For example, most homes spend about 12 percent of their income on groceries. This would include all items normally purchased at a grocery store, including office supplies, cleaning supplies, and other miscellaneous items. Although each household's budget will be different, this process can reveal areas in your finances that are causing difficulties.

- Examine where you are with consumer debt. When we speak of consumer debt, we are not talking about home mortgages or business loans. We are speaking of debt incurred to purchase items we consume. In other words, items that depreciate or lose value rapidly. This may include credit cards, vehicle loans, or family loans. Most families who have not paid attention to their finances end up struggling with consumer debt. As you try to determine your current financial situation, you will need to look closely at this. It is important to understand why you have used consumer debt, find a workable path out of it, and consider how to avoid it in the future.

If you have neglected your finances in the past, it will take some time and effort to get them organized. There is no simple shortcut. It is like letting the garden grow up in weeds. There is no way around some initial hard work. Many good budget plans and even software programs are available to help with this. If you have found one that works for you, stick with it.

A Word to the Discouraged

Before we move on to specifics of how you can take positive steps toward knowing where you are, I want to offer you a word of hope. All of this may seem overwhelming, and as you look at the current disorganized state of your finances, perhaps you are discouraged. Maybe looking at your situation is a little like Nehemiah looking at the ruins of Jerusalem.

You remember the story. He arrived in Jerusalem, and what he saw was simply a big mess. I don't know if he was prepared for what he saw or not. I don't know what he visualized as he worked day after day as the king's cupbearer, but I suspect he wasn't quite prepared for the reality of the destruction he faced when he arrived.

Perhaps you have this same fear. Maybe you have ignored your finances because you are afraid of how bad your state of affairs might be. But remember, even though your financial situation seems bleak, there is hope. Nehemiah's situation looked impossible too, but Nehemiah succeeded in his endeavor for two reasons.

1. He understood his own limitations and continually leaned upon God. We find this all through the story of Nehemiah. When opportunity came to tell the king of his concern, Nehemiah whispered a prayer. While planning the work, he asked God for direction. When threatened by enemies, he again talked to God. Throughout this seemingly impossible task, Nehemiah knew the task was larger than he could handle, so he kept giving it back to God.

2. The people had a mind to work.[a] Nehemiah didn't just tell God about the problem and then hope God would take care of it. The people were willing to work as the Lord provided direction and strength. This meant putting in some long hours. We don't read of any nice vacations during this time. They were willing to give up their wants and the life they had become accustomed to previously to achieve the goal of building the wall.

Both of these attributes are important if you are serious about recommitting your finances to God. No matter how great your past failure in this area may have been, if you are willing to ask for strength and direction from God and use the strength and direction He gives, there is hope!

Rise Up and Build!

I am always inspired as I read this account in Nehemiah. These people were surrounded by wreckage and debris and by enemies who taunted and tried to discourage them. But we can be encouraged by the words of the people that day. As they stood there in the middle of the mess, Nehemiah told them how God had prospered him and how God would be with them.

I don't know how I would have responded. It was a dismal scene as they stood there on the rubble of past failure. Yet, as Nehemiah laid out the vision, the people trusted God and said, "Let us rise up and build." Take courage from these words. As you begin the process of analyzing where you are, believe that God will be with you, and then in His strength, rise up and build!

---

[a]Nehemiah 4:6

Study Questions

1. Do you ever find yourself wanting to ignore financial issues? Why?

2. Why can money create barriers between a husband and wife? How can we avoid this?

3. Can you share a time in your life when you were discouraged with your finances? What steps did you take? What lessons did you learn?

4. Can you think of someone who has been faithful through a financial difficulty? If so, how has this example influenced your life?

5. Why do you think God wants us to work through financial concerns? Why didn't God just provide income for the Apostle Paul so he wouldn't have to stop preaching and work on tents?

CHAPTER SIX
What Is a Financial Statement?

Many times upon entering a mall or large department store, there will be a map of the building showing where the different stores or departments are. If Aunt Nelly has a birthday next week and you want to locate the Hallmark store, you look at the map and search for the appropriate section. After you have located Hallmark on the map, the next thing you need to know is where you are right now. Often there will be an arrow and the words "You are here." Once you know where you are and where Hallmark is located, it is easy to plot a direct course to Hallmark.

A financial statement, sometimes referred to as a statement of financial position, is a picture of where you currently are. It shows what you have in your checking accounts, savings accounts, and even in your wallet. It will also include the value of all the things you own—your home (if you own one), your car, furniture, lawnmower, etc. All these are known as your assets.

It will also include your liabilities. This will include the mortgage on your home, loans on vehicles, credit card debts, unpaid bills, etc. When all your liabilities are added up and subtracted from your total assets, you will come up with a number. This number represents your net worth. If all your possessions were sold and all your bills paid, this is the amount you would have. A financial statement simply says "You are here."

There are many good reasons to create a financial statement, but this process also has some pitfalls. We want to address both the rationale for a financial statement as well as ways to avoid a harmful focus.

Beware

Jesus said, "Take heed, and beware of covetousness: for a man's life consisteth not in the abundance of the things which he possesseth."[a] A financial statement is a way to calculate the things which you possess. If you enjoy sitting down and adding up the assets you have accumulated, be warned. God did not intend for your life, your fulfillment, or your inner strength to come from the abundance of material things. Life is to be found in Jesus Christ alone. If you find your mind continuing to go back over your list of financial assets, or if you find yourself measuring the worth of yourself or others by physical assets, beware! Jesus was very clear. Our worth as humans cannot be valued in dollars. The poorest street child in Calcutta is worth more than all the money, property, and things of this life.

Before we begin discussing the use of financial statements, we need to be aware that financial statements calculate the value of things which have no eternal value. Because of this, they can become a snare to us if used improperly or if too much thought and emphasis is given to them.

Using a Financial Statement Correctly

We have discussed the danger in an improperly used financial statement. Now we want to look at how one can help you. Following are several reasons why taking the time to fill out a financial statement can be beneficial.

- You may not be where you think you are. I have sat down with individuals who really thought they were doing well but, after filling out a financial statement, were shocked at how little they actually had. They had slowly accumulated debt by purchasing items having no long-term value. The item was gone, but they were still paying off the debt.

- It may affect how you make financial decisions in the future. Many items we purchase lose value instantly. Consider, for a moment, the purchase of a sofa. I decide to purchase a new sofa and am so excited to find just the one I wanted on sale. Last

[a]Luke 12:15

week it would have cost $900, but today it is on sale for only $799. Where I live we have an 8 percent sales tax, so this sofa will cost about $862, but this doesn't deter me since it would have cost even more last week.

After installing my newly purchased furniture in my living room and rejoicing over the good deal, I sit down to update my financial statement. Of course, I deduct the $862 that came out of my checkbook, but I have also added to the value of my home furnishings. How much have I added? I haven't added $862. Why not? Because the sofa is no longer worth $862. The value of this sofa is now whatever I can sell a used sofa for. Have you checked the classifieds for used sofas lately? I probably could not sell my sofa for more than $200 or $300. A financial statement will reveal to me that my new sofa just dropped my net worth around $500.

- Creating your own financial statement and taking the time to update it monthly for a period of time can be a great educational experience. It will teach the value in giving thought before buying, show which purchases are detrimental to your financial goals, and ultimately make you a more educated shopper.

- If you are having financial difficulty, updating your financial statement periodically can help you know if you are winning. If you are trying to climb out of consumer debt, your financial statement can become a scorecard, letting you know if you are successfully gaining back the ground you lost in the past.

- A financial statement can also help you plan for the future. If, for example, you have a long-term goal of purchasing your own home, a financial statement can help you decide if now is the right time to borrow money. If you have noticed that your net worth has been declining and income has not been keeping up with expenses, you may want to wait and take care of this problem before incurring debt and higher monthly payments.

Conclusion

A financial statement is just the beginning. This process does not provide all the information needed to start putting a budget together. It does not tell how much you have been earning or where your money has been going. But it is an important first step.

The importance of this concept is taught in the Bible. In Proverbs 27:23 the writer says, "Be thou diligent to know the state of thy flocks, and look well to thy herds." The writer goes on to explain why this is important: because "riches are not forever." In other words, life brings continual change, and we must occasionally give some thought to our current situation. Jesus also taught a similar principle when He said this: "For which of you, intending to build a tower, sitteth not down first, and counteth the cost, whether he have sufficient to finish it? Lest haply, after he hath laid the foundation, and is not able to finish it, all that behold it begin to mock him, Saying, This man began to build, and was not able to finish."[b]

While the primary teaching here is the importance of self-examination before deciding to follow Jesus, He is also saying it is wise to analyze where we are before launching out and pursuing a vision. A financial statement is one way we can do this.

Study Questions

1. What are the dangers of a financial statement? How can we know if we are using one improperly?

2. How can a financial statement help you make wise financial decisions?

3. Can you share a time when you made a purchase that turned out to be much more costly than you first thought? What did you learn from this?

4. How can a financial statement help if we are struggling with consumer debt?

5. What does a financial statement not tell you about your financial situation?

[b]Luke 14:28-30

CHAPTER SEVEN
Tracking Our Expenses

We had not been married long before we experienced the reality of financial strain. It seemed as though, no matter how we planned, there was never quite enough money to accomplish everything we wanted to do. I had always enjoyed keeping track of my finances as a young man, was confident I was good at it, and couldn't imagine ever surrendering this part of my life. But there was just one little fly in my ointment. My wife was better at record keeping than I was. It took some time for me to admit this, but truth became too evident to ignore.

I enjoyed strategizing. I loved to sit down with a calculator and project how money could be earned. But I had little patience for figuring out why the checkbook was off by $2.35. I would tell my wife, "Just throw a couple of dollars in and let's go to bed." My wife, on the other hand, was willing to stay up and make sure the checkbook was balanced. She wanted to know for sure that, if the bank statement said we had $187.56, our checkbook agreed. And many times there wasn't much more than that in there, by the way.

If you have any experience at all in keeping records, I don't need to tell you which of these methods works best. It took her several evenings to untangle the financial mess I had created before we were married. The offshoot of this little scenario was a husband who experienced great pride reduction, and a wife firmly established in the role of bookkeeper. This arrangement has worked well ever since, with one exception.

I began to experience what many husbands whose wives keep the books have experienced. As breadwinners, we go out and work hard to bring home a sufficient income. We want to be good providers; that is the role God has given us. We want our wives to admire us and view us as capable men—men who go out into the world and conquer. Men who are at least as good at providing an income as other men. Consequently, the size of the check we bring home is, in our minds, a reflection on our manhood.

I think most of us are happy with the check we bring home. We have worked hard, and it looks like a lot of money! Surely any normal family could live on this amount. So you can imagine how I felt after finding out there wasn't enough in the checkbook to cover all the bills. If you are a husband, you don't need to imagine. You are probably familiar with the feeling.

My first reaction to this dilemma was to blame my wife. After all, since I wasn't interested in questioning the size of my paycheck, all that was left to blame was my wife's bookkeeping and spending habits.

My wife and I experienced this conflict several times early in our marriage. I couldn't understand why she couldn't make our income work, and she didn't know how to stretch dollars any further than she already was. I didn't think she was being frugal enough, and she didn't believe I understood how much things really cost. Out of these periodic discussions came a decision that has blessed us tremendously throughout our married life. We decided to write down every single expense for one whole year. We wanted to find out where our money was really going.

This wasn't easy. For me, it meant carrying a small tablet in my front pocket. Every time I purchased a newspaper, Pepsi, or candy bar, I wrote down the cost. Anytime she bought some unneeded knickknack, she kept the receipt. We tried to carefully keep track of every penny. My wife then took a piece of paper, drew vertical lines on it, and began to add up what we had spent in each category each month. She was very detailed. If we paid fifty cents for parking, we wrote it down. Each time we stopped at Taco Bell, we wrote it down. And each item we wrote down was categorized separately. This way we could tell how much was spent each month on little items we hadn't thought much about in the past.

The Effect of Tracking

Choosing to agree with God that I am a steward and not an owner has had the greatest impact on my finances. It is a daily, sometimes hourly, choice, and I am still learning. But closely following this choice, one of the next greatest steps was the decision to track our expenses. I was not prepared for what this simple experiment would reveal about my life. I began to learn that operating a home was more expensive than I had realized, and balancing the budget for a household was more involved and difficult than I had wanted to admit. My wife was wisely silent, but I still suspect she secretly enjoyed this process.

I was also amazed how this process affected my view of cost. Suddenly items I had viewed as inexpensive and insignificant began to look different. Those occasional newspapers, which at the time only cost fifty cents, became much more expensive when I saw how much they added up to in a month. Stopping at McDonald's instead of packing a lunch isn't that significant when it only happens every other month. But when it is a daily occurrence, the impact on a budget can be significant.

I began to view the small items in a store in a new way. A bag of potato chips at $1 may not seem too expensive. Surely I can afford a bag of chips! But when I realize buying those chips every day can cost me several hundred dollars a year, a bag of chips begins to look amazingly overpriced. Suddenly some of my habitual purchases became less attractive, and I began to realize the price displayed in the store was not the true cost of the item. I wonder how truth in advertising would affect some businesses today. How well would Starbucks sell their mocha latte if the sign said, "Have one each day on the way to work and it will cost you only $1,123 a year"?

Those lunches at the fast food restaurant didn't look quite as attractive when I realized packing my lunch could have saved us over a

> **How well would Starbucks sell their mocha latte if the sign said, "Have one each day on the way to work and it will cost you only $1,123 a year"?**

hundred dollars that month. Our spending habits began to change as we came face to face with the fact that our own choices were creating our problem. But this discovery also gave us hope. It was encouraging to find that we were holding the steering wheel. There was something we could do, and it just involved little choices.

I encourage every young couple starting out in a new home to track their expenses for a year. I am convinced there are few things you could do that would be more beneficial. But it is important for both husband and wife to be involved in this process. As you spend time together writing down expenses and tabulating monthly totals, it will be much easier to identify problems and work on solutions later. In most marriages, it is the husband who resists addressing the family's finances, yet as the leader of the home, it is he who should be taking the initiative. But there is a reason we men resist. After all, agreeing to start writing down what I spend every day means admitting there is a slight possibility I might be part of the problem.

I Know What I Am Doing

It is the same reason I resist stopping to ask for directions on a road trip, even when the stores we drive past begin to look familiar. Stopping tells my wife I don't know where we are. So, as we drive past the same store for the third time, my wife patiently pretends she has never seen this area of town before. Years of financial struggle could be avoided in many homes if men would be humble enough to admit part of the blame lies with them.

There is another reason we men resist tracking expenses, and this is the simple fact that we share the responsibility for excessive spending. As men, we like to talk about women and their tendency to purchase unnecessary items like purses, shoes, knickknacks for the wall, and pretty little doilies for the table in the hall. Women do have difficulty leaving pretty things alone, and in some homes the wife can become a major obstacle to financial reform. A continual desire to redecorate can put tremendous financial strain on a household.

But men have their weaknesses too. They tend to get involved in hobbies like hunting and fishing, or woodworking and fixing up old cars. We are afraid to begin tracking expenses due to fear of what might be revealed. There are a couple of interesting points about the hobbies men usually get involved in.

- Men tend to buy items that are more expensive. While women are inclined to buy unnecessary items more frequently, the purchases men make are generally much larger. Many men who complain about their wives' spending habits have their closets full of shotguns, fishing rods, or other toys for the hobbies they enjoy. It is difficult for a wife to listen to criticism regarding her home-decorating weakness when there is a new bass boat in the driveway. It is hard for a wife to understand why she should economize when her husband, who loves woodworking or tinkering on vehicles, is constantly bringing home more tools. These items are generally expensive and can add up to much more than the smaller unnecessary items purchased by women.

- Men believe their hobbies are defendable. A man can explain how the hobby he enjoys puts meat in the freezer or produces an occasional chair or table. If his wife points to the cost of the hobby, the husband defends the expense by pointing out that his hobby produces something. There is nothing inherently wrong in any of these hobbies. There are good reasons to go fishing. But couples need to be honest, and tracking expenses is the only way to really know how much per pound we're paying for those fish.

But It Was on Sale

Many women would also be amazed if they would total the cost of grocery store purchases that were not on their original lists. If each time they returned from the store they would write down all the items purchased that were not really necessary, but "just happened to be on sale," many would be surprised. They might also be surprised at their fabric inventory. Shopping for more fabric can be used to justify recreational shopping.

Several years ago I was in a Third World market with another couple I had known for many years. I had been impressed with their attempt at Kingdom living. They had lived an affluent lifestyle in the past, but in recent years had chosen to commit their resources to building the Kingdom. As we walked through the market, we came to a section where dress material was sold. As the wife admired some of the inexpensive fabric, one of the pieces caught her attention, and she quietly mentioned to her husband, "I like this one." I don't think they knew I could hear them, but the short discussion that followed impressed me.

The husband responded, "Yes, it is a nice piece of fabric, but you already have a number of good dresses at home." The wife looked at the fabric a little longer and as she put it back said, "You are right. I don't need more dresses." What impressed me wasn't the fact that they didn't buy the fabric. I was inspired by their example of stewardship and their ability to communicate as a couple regarding their vision. Stewardship and Kingdom building had moved from being just a nice topic of discussion to an overriding vision that was being implemented even in small choices.

Learning From Tracking

John had grown up in another area, and he was still learning to live on his own. He moved into our community during a time when many single young men came to work through the summer. Many of them came desiring the freedom to make their own choices and to try living on their own. After some time had passed, John stopped in one day and said he wanted to talk about his finances.

After discussing the importance of budgeting (something John had never tried) and some inquiry about credit cards (something John had tried), we decided to take some time to track his expenses. I sent some materials home with John so he could categorize his past expenses, gave him some instruction on how he could begin analyzing his on-going costs, and set a time to meet with him again. John had also accumulated some debt, so we discussed the importance of curtailing expenses so some of this debt could be repaid.

John and I began meeting on a regular basis, and I began to notice a recurring pattern in one area of his expenses. Almost every week he had some expenses listed under clothing. I didn't think much about it at first, but as time went on, I became more concerned. We were trying to find extra money to go toward repaying debt, and since money kept flowing toward clothing, I finally confronted John. I asked him if some clothing he had recently purchased was really needed.

After some discussion John confessed he really had no need for more clothing. He had just walked through a store and seen some items he liked, so he had purchased them. I went back to some previous clothing purchases, and when I asked about those expenses, I received the same reply. "No, I probably didn't need to buy those shirts, but I was walking through the store and liked them, so I bought them." It looked like this young man, who was carrying a good-sized debt load, was making poor choices.

I asked how long he could go without spending any money on clothes before others would notice. I was shocked by his answer. John said he currently had enough clothes in his closet to last him for a long time. In fact, he was sure that if he stopped buying clothes now, he could go for five years without buying any more and none of his friends would even notice! So we went back over John's records, looking at how much was being spent on clothing. We discovered he was spending over a hundred dollars each month on clothing he didn't need.

Now John was the one who was surprised. He had no idea this much money was going into his clothes-buying habit. He had just bought a little here and there, but tracking had revealed the actual cost to him. As we continued to discuss his situation, John became aware that shopping for him was more about buying acceptance than purchasing clothing. It had also become a way to forget rejection. If he was not invited to an event or felt shunned in some way, he found relief from pain in shopping. After praying about the problem, he agreed to buy no clothing for a length of time and asked for accountability. Tracking his expenses had revealed an area that was out of balance, and it had revealed an inner deficiency more important than the expense.

Conclusion

If you are struggling financially or having difficulty reaching financial goals you have set, I appeal to you. Sit down with your spouse and discuss tracking. It takes some time and commitment, but you will find that doing this as a couple will be revealing and invaluable in your pursuit of Biblical stewardship. This is not a practice that needs to be continued indefinitely in most homes. But committing to track every dollar for a period of time and faithfully following through can be an educational, eye-opening experience.

Study Questions

1. Have you tried tracking expenses in your home? What did you learn?

2. What are some frivolous items you tend to purchase regularly, forgetting the yearly effect on your finances?

3. What types of hobbies or activities tempt men in your setting? What types of hobbies or activities tempt women in your setting?

4. How much recreation or pursuit of hobbies is acceptable before God?

5. What positive or negative effect could tracking have on a marriage relationship?

CHAPTER EIGHT
Examining Our Past Spending

Many people who are trying to deal with their financial situations will ask, "How do I know if I am spending too much money in a particular area?" This is a good question, and everyone's life is a little different. If you live in New York City, for example, your housing costs are going to be much different from a family who lives in Plain City, Ohio. So it is difficult to set a dollar amount for a category like housing. But what we can do is look at the percentage of income that each type of expense should require.

For example, a man who lives in New York City may spend more for housing, but he also will bring home a larger income—at least he had better! So the percentage of income that is spent for housing could be similar, even though the expense may be much larger in one geographical area than in another.

Average Percentages Intended for the Struggling

It is important to note, before looking at percentages, that these averages are intended for those who are having difficulty with their finances. They are not intended to soothe the conscience of a man whom the Holy Spirit is convicting. Maybe your house is paid for and some of your children are married. If so, the percentage of your income going toward housing should be much different than a young family just getting started.

With this understanding, let's look at a few categories of expenses and the average percentage of income each expense generally consumes. Again, these are just averages that financial advisers typically use and will differ somewhat depending on your situation. But they can help give a starting point in analyzing your tracking of expenses.

Giving

Christians give. It can be no other way, and increasing this portion of your budget as the years go by should be a primary goal. It should be discussed regularly and should affect your day-to-day decision making. Every budget should include giving to ensure it happens regularly. There needs to be a commitment to giving back to the Lord which exceeds our desire to satisfy the flesh. I am not going to suggest a percentage. All of us are aware that God asked His people to give 10 percent in the past. Perhaps this is what God will call you to, but I believe there are many among us who should be giving much more. Perhaps we should say 10 percent is a good place to start. The Lord will bless as we choose to give regularly, cheerfully, and sacrificially. It is the natural response of a heart that realizes every resource is unearned and undeserved.

Housing—38 Percent

This category is almost always the largest and therefore many couples have difficulty with it. This should include everything that goes into housing, including mortgage payments or rent, insurance, maintenance, and lawn care. At times this percentage must be raised, but just keep this fact in mind: an expense budget cannot total more than 100 percent, so anytime you spend more in one category, you must spend less in another.

Automotive—15 Percent

This category should include all costs pertaining to transportation, including insurance, taxes, and fuel. This should also include savings for depreciation on your vehicle so you are prepared for unexpected repairs and replacement.

Vehicles in America have come to represent more than just transportation. Our cars and trucks have become a projection of who we are. They speak of our status and success in life. Because of this, it is tempting to spend more on a vehicle than is actually warranted. This category, like housing, is a difficult one for young couples. But often the reason it is difficult is not because there are no economical options, but because we are more concerned about public perception than basic transportation. This is especially evident in young people, although it is certainly not confined to them. Having a Kingdom focus can be a great liberator from the pressure of society that surrounds us.

> **Having a Kingdom focus can be a great liberator from the pressure of society that surrounds us.**

Groceries—12 Percent

Food costs will vary greatly with the size and age of your family. Choices at the grocery store, such as whether or not you buy prepared foods and how often you have meat in your diet, will have a noticeable effect on this portion of your budget. Many families use their gardens to provide a large percentage of their food. This not only saves on food costs but also provides a way for children to contribute. Another factor that will affect this percentage is the number of guests you entertain. One of the reasons hospitality becomes costly and is sometimes neglected in our homes is due to the level of expectation we create. I enjoy sitting down to a table where thought and effort have been given to a meal. But when our wives neglect hospitality due to the expectations we put on them, something is wrong. When food, rather than fellowship, becomes the focal point, a wife can feel unnecessary pressure. I have greatly appreciated being in some young couples' homes where the meal is simple and inexpensive.

The grocery portion of a budget should include not only food, but also anything you would normally purchase at the supermarket.

Clothing—5 Percent

I know several young families who purchase a large percentage of their clothing at thrift shops and garage sales. By purchasing used clothing, they are able to save substantially. However, discretion must be used. We are not interested in sacrificing simplicity or modesty to balance a budget, but many good coats, shirts, and shoes can be purchased secondhand. If we are serious about debt reduction or really interested in finding ways to increase our giving, this is one place it can be done.

Sometimes young mothers struggle with peer pressure as they decide what kind and how much clothing to buy for their children. It is easy to feel we must keep up with the mother in our congregation who always has a new outfit for her children. But there is great peace in following simplicity in dress. You will not only bless your children, but you will also bless your congregation. Your decisions will provide either positive or negative peer pressure for the families that surround you. And of course, avoiding name-brand and fashionable clothing will also help your budget.

> **Your decisions will provide either positive or negative peer pressure for the families that surround you.**

Recreation and Travel—3 Percent

Many families are unrealistic with this category when formulating a budget, but it should not be overlooked. Few of us stay at home all the time, and travel is sometimes necessary. This category could also include gift-giving and hobbies such as fishing, hunting, and sports equipment. By setting some money aside for these types of expenses, we can be better prepared when we need to attend a funeral or wedding in another area.

Medical—7 Percent

This category, too, will greatly vary. If you are older, 7 percent may not be enough, and for some families this may be excessive. If you have some type of insurance or plan that shares the cost, it is easier to project what your monthly cost will be. If you do not have any insurance, or if your congregation has agreed to share medical costs among yourselves, you may want to consider setting aside a certain percentage each month in anticipation of these expenses.

School

This is another expense that varies greatly with each family. It is generally a fixed amount each month, if your children go to a private school, so it is simple to arrive at the percentage you will need to budget. If your children are taught at home, there may be a large expense once or twice a year. This total amount can be divided by twelve and saved each month so you are ready when the larger expenses are due.

Miscellaneous—5 Percent

This category is designed to cover items that do not fit anywhere else. This would include expenses like haircuts or subscriptions to magazines. This category can also be used when an emergency in another area of the budget causes insufficient funds in that category.

Conclusion

As we conclude this section, several points need to be reiterated.

- The percentages listed above are only given to help you analyze where you are. Every situation is different, and every budget will be different. It is important that these percentages not be used as ammunition between marriage partners. It is easy for a husband to suspect that his wife is not being as frugal as she should be and use these suggested percentages to prove it. They are not given for this purpose.

- It is important to remember that the total list of percentages of expenses in your budget must not add up to more than 100 percent. If there is more going out than coming in, something must be changed.

- The percentages given above do not deal with consumer debt. If you have credit card debt, one of the percentages above must get smaller. In other words, you may need to reduce the amount you are spending in Recreation and Travel or Groceries to help pay off your debt. This topic will be addressed again in the section on consumer debt.

Study Questions

1. How should a couple determine what percentage to give? What are the advantages of having a set percentage? What are the disadvantages?

2. Can you share about a time when you have been tempted to make choices based on peer pressure when buying a vehicle?

3. Do wives in your congregation feel pressure to serve expensive meals when entertaining visitors? If so, how could this pressure be reduced?

4. Discuss other ways we pressure each other in the area of vehicles, dress, vacations, etc.

5. If you currently have a budget, which of the categories do you have the most difficulty staying within?

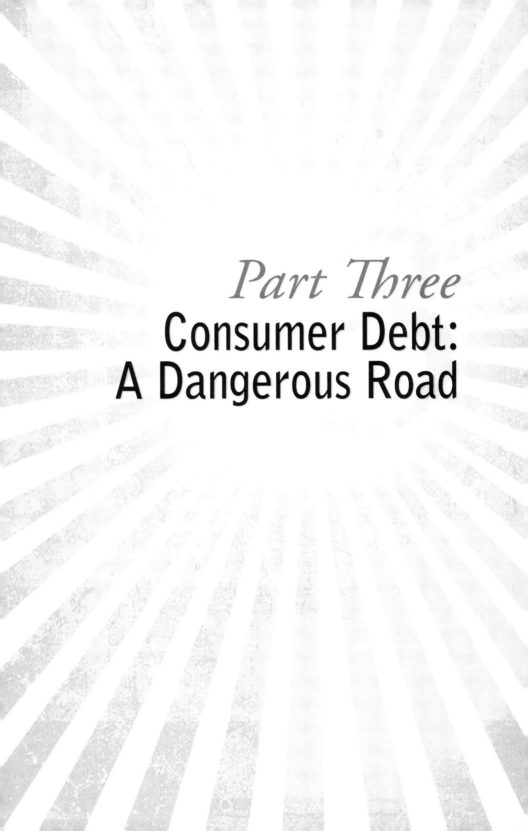

Part Three
Consumer Debt:
A Dangerous Road

Chapter Nine
The Illusion

Bob and Julie were well known within their Midwestern community and church family for having a deep love for the Lord and embracing strong family values. They always attended church functions and volunteered readily when help in the community was needed. They exhibited, both in word and deed, a love for the lost. Their children respected them, and anyone looking on had to be impressed by the obvious love shown between family members.

Bob was self-employed and had been successful in business. Although business was not his first love, it was evident that he had succeeded financially. They owned a nice home, drove respectable vehicles, and were hospitable and willing to share with others what the Lord had given them. In short, Bob and Julie had the type of family all of our Anabaptist communities need more of. They were the ideal family.

But underneath this beautiful picture was an unseen problem. Bob and Julie were deep in consumer debt. They had gradually, over a period of years, taken on more and more credit card, vehicle, and personal debt. No one in their local church family would have suspected it. They attended church services just as faithfully as the others. They sang with the same enthusiasm, joined in group discussions like everyone else, and always had a good word to say about the sermon.

Their problem wasn't evident to the surrounding community. They were always available to help their neighbors and enjoyed sharing the good news of the Gospel with whoever would listen. Bob was the type of person you could call if you needed help. Julie loved to bake and had a reputation for dropping off a loaf of bread to someone who was struggling.

Their children didn't know there was a problem either. They had never thought of their parents as extravagant or wasteful. Their mother and father had always provided what was needed and taught them to be thankful for what the Lord had blessed them with. The children lived happily day by day, never suspecting the lifestyle they so much enjoyed was threatened by a ticking time bomb called consumer debt.

But perhaps the most alarming fact in this little account is that Bob and Julie were oblivious to reality as well. Consumer debt had, ever so slowly, wrapped its deceitful tentacles around their lives. Many little choices had been made along the way—decisions that sounded good at the time and made life easier at the moment. But suddenly they were faced with the reality that interest on consumer debt was consuming a significant portion of their income, and they were having difficulty making even the minimum payments on their growing debt.

Bob and Julie never intended to arrive at this point. They never imagined this could happen to them. In their earnest desire to focus on serving the Lord rather than the materialistic chase that surrounded them, they had neglected budgeting and Biblical financial stewardship. They had failed to understand that serving the Lord does not mean ignoring money; rather, being sold out to Jesus Christ is a call for commitment in every part of our lives, including finance. It must be pointed out that

> **. . . being sold out to Jesus Christ is a call for commitment in every part of our lives, including finance.**

in Bob and Julie's story, as well as in all of our situations, consumer debt is not the real trouble. Consumer debt is a symptom of the real problem—an indicator of a greater underlying concern.

Defining Consumer Debt

When we speak of consumer debt, we are not talking about home mortgages or business loans. We are speaking of debt that is incurred to purchase items we consume—items that depreciate or lose value rapidly. For example, you may choose to purchase a home that costs $150,000, but you expect that home to be worth at least $150,000 when you finally finish paying off the loan fifteen or thirty years later. This is why home loans are not considered consumer debt. Homes do not lose value rapidly; in fact, they normally gain value over time.

On the other hand, when you stop at your local ice cream shop and purchase an ice cream cone, you know you are purchasing something that will lose most of its value in a short period of time. If you choose to charge the cost of this ice cream to your credit card and make the minimum payment on your card, you will be paying for it long after it has lost its value. Ice cream is an item that rapidly depreciates. Typically we use consumer debt to purchase items we do not have the money to pay for now. We don't have the money, but we still want the item. Why do we do this? One reason is that consumer debt is deceitful.

The Illusion of Consumer Debt

Growing up in the Central Valley of California, I was surrounded by migrant workers. Many of them could not speak English, yet due to the need for agricultural labor, they were a necessary part of the community and were accepted as such. As I mingled with these young Hispanics during my high school years, I observed a common trait. Many of them lived in small houses that looked nearly uninhabitable. Several families would share these little houses in an attempt to cut down on rent, and many of them lived very frugally so they could send money back to their families in Mexico.

But the interesting pattern I observed among the second generation children who had never actually lived in Mexico was their obsession with vehicles. While their parents had lived frugally so they could send extra money back home, these young people would buy cars on credit and then embellish the vehicles with all kinds of lights and trinkets. On the weekends they could be seen driving slowly through town, wanting to see and be seen. Their cars became their identities. They still lived in shacks. But as they cruised up and down the main drag of town, they pretended to be wealthy. They were temporarily finding enjoyment in an illusion of wealth.

Those of us who were not part of the Hispanic community used to scoff at the ridiculousness of it. It seemed crazy to park a dressed-up car in front of a tumble-down house. Why couldn't they see the inconsistency?

But not many years later, I was smitten with the realization that I was doing the same thing. As a young man, I had borrowed money to buy a nice car. There were cars available I could have paid cash for, but I was willing to take out a loan, pay interest, and pay more insurance simply because of what others might think. I wanted others to believe I was successful and could afford something this nice. I was using consumer debt to create an illusion.

An Illusion of Wealth

Most of us who have credit cards can remember when we received the first one. Maybe it had a $2,000 credit limit, and walking around with that in our pocket felt great. Suddenly lots of things were within our grasp. Things that just a week earlier we couldn't afford were now available. We suddenly felt rich!

But had anything actually changed in our financial status? Did we actually have more money now? No, we did not have any more assets now than we had the week before. The credit card was providing an illusion of wealth. Credit card companies and stores have long understood this. That is why department stores continue to issue their own credit cards. They know a consumer will spend more in their store if he is using a card.

Few individuals are not influenced by this illusion of wealth. Most people believe credit cards have no effect on how they make purchases, but statistics show otherwise. Statistics vary, but estimates show that the average consumer spends approximately 18 percent more when using a credit card than he does when paying with cash. We tend to weigh purchases more cautiously when using cash, a little less cautiously when writing checks, and not very thoughtfully when paying with credit cards.

I think it is good for all of us to look closely

> " . . . estimates show that the average consumer spends approximately 18 percent more when using a credit card than he does when paying with cash. "

at this truth. You may not think you are affected adversely by consumer debt because you pay off your credit cards at the end of each month. But you may be spending more than necessary simply due to the ease of using credit cards.

The "It's Not That Much More" Illusion

There is another way we tend to be deceived by consumer debt. When I walk into our local appliance store to look for a new refrigerator, I am faced with many options. Some models are basic refrigerators, and others come with an assortment of bells and whistles. Some have painted finishes, and some are clad in stainless steel. There are refrigerators with more shelves, ice makers, ice and water in the door, and myriads of other options. Now imagine this scenario.

You need to purchase a refrigerator, and you have $1,400 in your checking account. You walk up to the display, and there in front of you are two refrigerators. The first is a basic model with an ice maker. The tag says it costs $899. Next to this refrigerator is one that not only has an ice maker, but also dispenses ice and water in the door. The price on this one is $1,149. You have always wanted an ice dispenser in the door, but you wonder if having ice and water in the door is really worth $250 more. As you weigh the convenience of having an outside dispenser against the extra cost, it seems like a lot of money for something so unnecessary. The other issue weighing on your mind is your checkbook. If you purchase the more expensive one, it would almost drain your checkbook, while choosing the less expensive one would leave more cash available.

Now imagine the same scenario, only in this situation you do not have the cash and plan to make monthly payments on the refrigerator. The plain-Jane refrigerator has a price tag informing you it can be purchased for $49 per month, while the refrigerator with ice and water will cost you $58 per month. For only $9 more per month, you can have the added feature of ice and water in the door. Marketers know it is much easier for the average consumer to agree to an additional $9 per month to get the refrigerator they really want than it is to shell out another $250 on the spot. This is an illusion. The individual who is willing to pay an additional $9 per month will usually spend much more than $250 over the term of the loan.

This is why we have seen an exponential increase in options on products as the use of credit has increased. It is easier for stores to sell extra options when people do not have to pay for them up front. Somehow, a little more each month doesn't bother us like an initial lump sum. It is an illusion, and marketers understand this. Let's look at another marketing illusion used today.

The Illusion of Tomorrow

"No Payments – No Interest for Six Months"

Marketing schemes like this one greet us almost every time we open the mail or read a newspaper. Several asterisks usually surround these statements, and if you take the time to read the fine print at the bottom (most people don't), you will generally find you are required to pay in full by the end of the term or face major penalties (many people do). This type of marketing has been very successful and is based on the premises that, first, people do not have enough money to buy the product; and second, people assume tomorrow will be better.

Each day brings its own set of challenges and problems. As we look ahead, we cannot anticipate what those troubles will be. God in His mercy has not burdened us with all the struggles coming our way in the next day, week, month, or year. So when the washing machine breaks down unexpectedly and a couple is trying to decide whether to buy a used one from the classifieds or a new one with state-of-the-art features, marketing like this is very tempting. Why not go ahead and buy the new washing machine and pay for it later when things aren't so tight?

But they are unaware that the transmission on their older minivan is going to give out in two months, the refrigerator is going to die within five months, and the boss is going to call during this time and say a job he thought they had just fell through. Suddenly the purchase of a washing machine has changed from a nice short-term plan of paying it off when things got better to a long-term payment plan.

In my area snowmobiling is the rage. Each fall our newspapers advertise the latest. It seems each year they have larger engines, better tracks, and new gadgets that were not available the year before. Suddenly the snowmobile that was state-of-the-art last fall is not even worthy to be compared with the new model. Many who love snowmobiling change models every couple of years to keep up.

The advertisements that continually pour into our homes attempting to sell these snowmobiles use this "tomorrow will be better" type of marketing. These "No Payments for Six Months" advertisements appear in December just as the snow begins to fall. A color picture shows the latest machine plowing through a couple feet of powder, and to the young man who can't look at the picture without experiencing rapid heartbeat, the offer is music to his ears. He can see himself flying up through the pine trees, the envy of his friends, and best of all, there are "No Payments for Six Months."

As he sits there looking at the picture, visualizing the possibilities and imagining the roar of this new and improved engine, he is probably forgetting that winter will end. There is nothing quite like the beginning of summer, with fishing and camping and all kinds of outdoor possibilities. But imagine, for a moment, this young man walking out to the mailbox on a beautiful, sunny June day and finding a statement informing him that his first payment is due on his snowmobile! He had forgotten all about this, and who wants to make snowmobile payments in June? He was getting excited about that new Jet Ski he just bought. But perhaps he shouldn't be too concerned. After all, no payments are due on the Jet Ski until December!

Conclusion

In this chapter we have looked at some of the ways we can be deceived by consumer debt. Consumer debt creates an illusion and is deceptive by its very nature. It unrealistically depends on life being better tomorrow, insinuates you are wealthier than you really are, and hides the true cost of a purchase. This "buy now, pay later" way of life can provide instant gratification, but at the expense of long-term financial stability.

Much of our trouble with consumer debt could be avoided if we were simply more patient. That inner desire to have what we want now can push us to make hasty decisions that become a snare to us for years to come. Marketers are conscious of the illusion created by consumer debt. Their goal is to sell their product, and they have found consumer debt to be an effective tool. But a healthy dose of skepticism can be helpful in the marketplace. Watch for the asterisks and the fine print. As financial advisers have taught for many years, "If it sounds too good to be true, it probably is!"

> **If it sounds too good to be true, it probably is!**

Study Questions

1. Bob and Julie had a deep desire to serve the Lord and were not spending for frivolous items. Why did they end up in such a financial crisis?

2. What are some areas in our lives where we attempt to live an illusion? When are we tempted to borrow to impress others?

3. Discuss the illusion of wealth created by credit. Do you find it easier to spend when using credit? How about when you are using a check? How about cash?

4. Can you share an experience in which you were enticed to purchase an item that was more expensive simply because it wasn't much more per month?

5. Can you share a time when the "buy now, pay later" sales pitch persuaded you to make an unwise decision?

CHAPTER TEN
The Danger

I was working in our backyard one beautiful day in June, trying to finish a little project, when my phone rang. It was a brother from another congregation whom I will refer to as Jim. Jim had been having financial difficulties, and we had talked a few times in the past. Jim's optimism had always impressed me. Somehow, even in the middle of the current crisis, he had always been able to see the hand of the Lord in the struggle. As I had talked to Jim from time to time, I had often come away from the discussions with a sense of guilt. Why couldn't I trust the Lord as Jim did? I had seen him make phone calls to lending agencies, trying to secure better terms for the massive debt he had incurred over time. He had often called me afterward, so excited that he had been able to share his faith in the Lord with the person on the phone that he forgot about his failure to alter the terms of his loan. Several times I had told my wife that, after talking to Jim about his financial problems, I was the one who couldn't sleep, not Jim!

But this time Jim's voice didn't sound the same on the phone. He sounded very concerned. Jim had just received a statement from a credit card company, and he had just happened to notice they had changed the interest rate. The rate had been 9 percent last month, and this month they had raised it to 27.5 percent. He had never been late making a payment on this card, and Jim couldn't understand why they had raised his rate. Further, with his precarious financial condition and the high balance he was carrying on this card, he was afraid this added monthly interest would tip him over the edge. As he investigated the reason for the dramatic increase in interest rate, he discovered in the fine print that the credit card company had the right to change his rate if his credit score changed. In other words, if he made a late payment on another card (which he had done), it could affect the terms of this card.

Many Americans are suddenly realizing a startling Biblical truth: The borrower is still servant to the lender. It is amazing how quickly the same companies that advertise credit with smiling faces can turn on you if things don't turn out according to the fine print. Americans are up in arms over credit card company rates, fees, and tactics. President Obama, in April 2009, much to the public's delight, even reprimanded the presidents of Visa and MasterCard at the White House.

Some of these companies have engaged in questionable marketing strategies. But are the credit card companies really to blame for all this? Shouldn't some of the blame rest on the shoulders of the consumer? Did anyone force us to run up these excessive balances? Perhaps our addiction to consumer debt is simply a reflection of our lack of contentment. Consider the following facts regarding America's consumer debt from the Federal Reserve Debt Statistics:

- Total consumer debt multiplied nearly five times from 1980 ($355 billion) to 2001 ($1.7 trillion). Consumer debt in 2008 stood at $2.6 trillion.

- The average household in 2008 carried nearly $8,500 in credit card debt.

The American Census Bureau estimates there are over 164 million credit card holders in the United States, and each credit card holder has an average of nine credit cards.

Credit has become a way of life in America. A few years ago I worked with a painter who readily voiced his opinion regarding consumption. "If I want something," he stated, "I just get it. I will pay later. It's the American way!" "Buy now, pay later" is the cry of the day; consequently, businesses, governments, and individual consumers are staggering under a mountain of debt.

Plain Churches Are Not Exempt

We could hope that this rush toward consumer debt only exists within the society that surrounds us, but this is not true. Most of us are aware of individuals within our Plain circles who have fallen into the trap of consumer debt. In an article on consumer debt, the *Calvary Messenger* made this statement:

> The incidence of out-of-control spending via credit cards is increasing. The situation now requires some straight talk. Examples could be cited of members in our Beachy churches with credit card debt from $40,000 to $220,000. People in these higher debt ranges have been using as many as twenty (and even more) cards.[5]

The Danger of Debt

Because we were surrounded by a peach orchard during my childhood in California, one of my jobs was to help irrigate. At that time irrigation was accomplished by opening a large valve at one end of the orchard and letting the water flood the field. To keep the water within the orchard, we built levies around the field. These dirt levies were about eighteen to twenty-four inches high, and great care was taken to make sure there were no gaps in the levies. As a boy, one of my responsibilities was to walk around the field and make sure the water was staying within the levy. You'd think that once the levies were in place you could relax; after all, what could go wrong? It would seem that, short of a tractor breaking down a levy, nothing could happen.

But our greatest fear wasn't big tractors. Our greatest foe was a tiny creature known as a gopher. Gophers were notorious for digging through levies. In a short time, a gopher could penetrate a levy, making a hole about 1½ inches in diameter. This hole shouldn't have created much concern, but the soil in our area was sandy loam, and within minutes a 1½-inch hole could grow to a large break in the levy. Just a small trickle could quickly transform into an unstoppable hemorrhage.

When this occurred, there was always great excitement. We dropped whatever we were doing and ran to the spot. Time was of the essence. The only way to stop a large flow like this was to place something (usually a panel of plywood or metal) in the break and shovel dirt around it. After the flow was stopped, the panel could be removed. If no panel was readily available, someone had to lie down in the gap

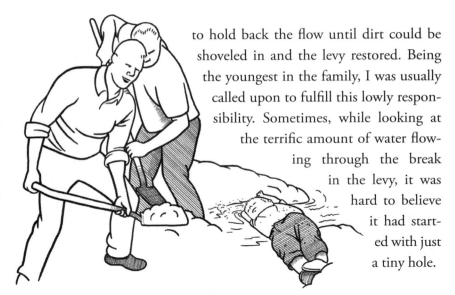

to hold back the flow until dirt could be shoveled in and the levy restored. Being the youngest in the family, I was usually called upon to fulfill this lowly responsibility. Sometimes, while looking at the terrific amount of water flowing through the break in the levy, it was hard to believe it had started with just a tiny hole.

We'll Pay It Off Next Month

Consumer debt has many similarities to the gopher hole. It looks so insignificant and harmless in the beginning. It starts small and sounds reasonable, but unless it is dealt with quickly, it can create catastrophic consequences. In almost every situation, consumer debt is not a result of planning to fail, but rather the consequence of failing to plan. I have never heard of anyone who planned on having long-term credit card debt, yet our society is plagued by it.

There are two primary reasons individuals find themselves drowning in consumer debt. Sometimes they encounter circumstances over which they have no control—perhaps a young couple has a medical situation or a sudden loss of income. The only way to function short term is to charge the immediate necessities. In these situations it is difficult for a family to know what to do. It might be better to contact someone they trust for counsel, even though this can be difficult or embarrassing.

The second scenario, which is far more common, is simply excessive spending. Without question, this is the primary cause of consumer debt in our homes. Many times unnecessary spending is the beginning of consumer debt, and then an emergency speeds the progression toward major crisis and long-term struggle.

So how can you know if credit cards are not a blessing to you? What signs indicate a problem? As a young man helping with irrigation, I looked for the first trickle of water. We didn't wait to act until we saw a raging torrent flowing out of a field. We wanted to stop the problem while it was small. So what should we look for in our finances? We want to examine a few signs that reveal a coming crisis in your personal finances. As you consider these indicators, be honest. Don't wait to act until the problem is massive.

- You are using a credit card because you do not have enough money in your checking account. Buying items you do not currently have enough money to pay for is an indicator that something is wrong.

- You receive a credit card bill you are unable to pay in full. This should be an early warning alert. This tells you that you have been spending more than you are bringing in. Remember, the debt is not the primary problem. The problem is the lifestyle creating the debt.

- Your credit card debt is increasing. If you have consumer debt, take a piece of paper and add up all the balances you have right now. Then compare the total to last month and the month before that. If your total debt is increasing, it is a sign you need to act immediately.

- You are only paying the minimum payment each month. This is a sure sign you are in trouble. It will take many years to pay off some of these cards if you are only paying the minimum payment. And remember, more unexpected financial situations are coming your way. This is just how life is. If you are so strapped that you can only make minimum payments, the only way to deal with unexpected expenses is to put them on a card, which increases the problem.

- You are hoping another credit card shows up in the mailbox. If you have reached the point where another credit card seems to be your only hope, your problem is massive. You will never get out of a hole by continuing to dig, and neither can you borrow your way out of debt.

If one of these symptoms applies to you, don't wait to take action. Regardless of what you are being told by our culture, ongoing consumer debt is neither normal nor necessary. The quicker you can get out from under its curse, the better off you will be.

Conclusion

Possibly at this point you are discouraged. Maybe all the bulleted points above apply to you. Perhaps you have reached a point where getting out of debt looks impossible. Before leaving this section, I want to give you a word of encouragement. The list of symptoms above describes the lives of many individuals. But if you are in this situation, take courage. Many people have found themselves up to their eyebrows in debt, yet have recovered and live debt-free today. If you have gradually accumulated debt, don't expect it to suddenly disappear. Be skeptical of any program that promises immediate deliverance. It will take prayer, diligence, resolve, and persistence to win the battle over consumer debt—but it is possible.

Study Questions

1. The borrower is still servant to the lender. Discuss some potential problems for a believer who is trying to be a servant of Jesus Christ and a servant of Visa at the same time.

2. Why are our Plain churches having the same struggles with consumer debt that our society has?

3. Is the credit card problem in our churches primarily a financial problem or a spiritual problem?

4. Why is it so important to act quickly when dealing with credit card problems?

5. Can you relate personal experiences or think of other individuals who have recovered from a bad financial situation? What was the key to their success?

CHAPTER ELEVEN

Deceptive Deliverance

As of June 2008, consumer debt in the United States stood at 2.6 trillion dollars. This works out to about $8,500 for every man, woman, and child living in the country.[6] Maybe this doesn't amaze you, but remember, this figure does not include mortgages, business loans, commercial real estate, etc. This statistic includes only consumer debt. Americans are sadly addicted to their car loans and credit cards, and millions are drowning in a sea of debt. They watch envelopes with little windows pour into their mailboxes each month, and many are becoming alarmed. As interest, administrative fees, and various creative charges rain down on top of the debt they have already amassed, fear sets in. Compounding finance charges create a compounding problem and ultimately overwhelming anxiety and panic.

On July 29, 2008, Emilio Saladriagas walked into a Rent-a-Center store in Bloomfield, New Jersey. Rent-a-Center rents furniture, electronics, and other goods with the option of eventually buying them, and Emilio was one of their customers. He was in desperate financial trouble, was behind on payments, and had become extremely frustrated by the high volume of late payment notices and collection phone calls he was receiving. He arrived at the store angry and agitated and asked to speak to the manager. When Emilio was told the manager was not available, he snapped. It was the last straw. Grabbing a bottle of lighter fluid, he poured it over his body and set himself on fire.

Emilio lived through the incident thanks to employees who quickly extinguished the blaze, but he was critically injured.[7]

In Debt and Desperate

Suicides and desperate acts by individuals overwhelmed by consumer debt are on the rise. Even youth are not immune. In June 2006 a documentary film titled *Maxed Out* was introduced to the public. The documentary was intended to warn parents of college students about the danger of heavy credit card use on college campuses, and more specifically, to increase awareness that debt is driving students to suicide. Students, many times without their parents' knowledge, are using consumer debt to fund their pursuit of acceptance while in school. Finally their mountain of debt looks impossible to overcome, and rather than admit to their peers and family they have failed, they take their own lives.

Admittedly, these examples of desperation are not the norm in our Anabaptist circles. Yet there is a warning here that we do not want to miss. Individuals who have acquired consumer debt can have a difficult time admitting their failure to others and have a tendency to resort to means they would not ordinarily consider. They feel squeezed by the increasing pressure as they receive warning letters and phone calls from collection agencies, and they start looking for some type of relief—a quick fix that will salvage their respect in the community. Sadly, many options are being marketed today that promise immediate relief, but are deceptive.

The purpose of this chapter is to address some of these deceptive and unethical methods. Some of these advertised offers are not advisable because they do not address the real problem. In other words, they will not really provide lasting assistance. Other methods should be avoided because they use tactics that are not compatible with basic Scriptural principles. Just because something works does not always mean it is acceptable.

The writer in Proverbs said a long time ago, "Give me neither poverty nor riches . . . Lest I be full, and deny thee, and say, Who

> **Just because something works does not always mean it is acceptable.**

is the LORD? or lest I be poor, and steal, and take the name of my God in vain."[a] He was acknowledging that certain situations provide strong temptations, and he was asking that the Lord would keep him from

[a]Proverbs 30:8-9

them. Whether we are deep in consumer debt or trying to help someone who is, we need to understand that the temptation to resort to questionable methods is real. Let's look at some of these methods of deceptive deliverance.

Illegal Scams

Due to millions of individuals struggling under a load of consumer debt, a huge opportunity has developed in America for scam artists. One of the methods used is convincing people they don't really owe the money. The argument is that credit card companies only lend credit, not real money, and therefore have no right to demand anything from you. You do not have any obligation to repay what the company says you owe, since there was no money legally lent to start with.

These scam artists give you the impression that credit card companies do not want this knowledge to come to light, and if you will just pay the debt reduction company a percentage of the debt, they will negotiate with the lender and your debt will disappear. This is, of course, a lie. It will only result in the debt reduction company walking off with cash, and you will be left with a larger debt than you had before. This "No Money Lent" scam, only one of the many scams in existence, has deceived many.

Legal but Unscriptural Methods

"Eliminate up to 70 Percent of Your Debt Now!"

"Have Your Credit Card Debt Terminated!"

"Stop Those Phone Calls — Let Us Dramatically Reduce Your Debt!"

Debt reduction has turned into a major business in America, and one cannot open any major newspaper or magazine without seeing advertisements like these. One would assume, from the wording, that these companies have a great desire to help you and your family. But what do these companies actually do? How can a company reduce your debt by 70 percent? Is it legal? Are Scriptural principles being violated?

One of the primary methods used by debt reduction companies is to force credit card companies to negotiate. In this scenario, you make an agreement with the debt reduction company, and they instruct you to stop making payments on your consumer debt. In other words, just ignore all those bills that keep coming in the mail. Obviously it won't be long until the phone begins to ring. When it does, you are instructed to inform your creditors that you have turned all your debt over to this debt reduction company.

This debt reduction company now begins to negotiate directly with your creditors from a position of power. They may say, "Look, my client is broke, and if you want to get anything at all from him, you will need to reduce his debt." This method is rarely as successful as advertised, but it often forces credit card companies to reduce the amount owed them.

Is this method acceptable in light of Scripture? Is it right to force a lender to accept less in return than what was borrowed?

God is very clear through both the Old and New Testaments that integrity with money is extremely important to Him. Are we really portraying integrity when we use a credit card to purchase an item that costs a hundred dollars and later try to force this creditor to accept fifty? These methods are legal but not Scriptural. There may be times when negotiation is needed to extend the term of a loan or ask for a reduced interest rate. But to use force to compel a lending institution to accept less than we borrowed violates Biblical principles.

Debt Consolidation

Another tempting option available today is known as debt consolidation. There are many different types of debt consolidation loans, and as the name implies, the goal is to consolidate or combine the many loans you now have into one. A reason for doing this may be to simplify your life. Why have loans to many different companies when you can simply write one check each month to one company?

Generally when we apply for a consolidation loan, we are trying to get relief from high monthly payments. A company can make this look attractive, but debt consolidation can be very deceptive. One of the problems is that debt consolidation almost always extends the term of the loan, which causes you to pay more interest over a longer period of time.

In addition to a longer term, some of these loans raise the interest rate. A consumer who is feeling strapped is generally only concerned about the net monthly payment. It is easy for him to sign up for a loan that provides short-term relief but long-term regret.

Remember, debt is not the primary problem. If lifestyle adjustment is not incorporated into your strategy, little will change. When a consolidation loan pays off all the credit card bills, these credit cards then become available for more purchases. Because of this, these types of loans can give false hope and do long-term damage. Loan consolidation can be beneficial in some situations, but only when coupled with a budget to restrict spending habits. Even in that case, counsel should be sought first.

Home Equity Loans

One of the often suggested and frequently advertised ways to quickly eliminate your consumer debt is to convert it into a home equity loan. Why pay 27 percent interest on a credit card balance when you can get a home equity loan for 8 percent? Let's look at why a higher interest loan with a shorter term can actually cost less.

Let's imagine you have $20,000 in credit card debt and the average interest on your cards is 25 percent. If you paid this debt off over a five-year period, you would need to pay $587 per month, or a total of $35,220.

Now let's assume you have an opportunity to refinance and pay off this debt with an 8 percent home equity loan. This loan would be spread out over thirty years and have a monthly payment of $147, for a total of $52,920 over the life of the loan. If you are only looking at the monthly payment, this looks pretty good. Who wouldn't want to exchange a $587 monthly payment for one that is only $147?

But if you back up and look at the long-term picture, you have just agreed to pay an additional $17,700 for this monthly relief over the next thirty years. Remember, it is important to consider length of loan when looking at options, as well as the rate of interest. It may be appropriate to consider a home equity loan, but don't be deceived. Home equity loans do not reduce or eliminate debt; they just move it around and stretch it out.

Conclusion

How can we know when an advertised program is deceptive? How can we be sure it will provide real relief? This book cannot address all the programs being advertised, but one word should raise a red flag. If you see this word used to describe a particular program, beware. This word is *easy.* Effective debt reduction is never easy. It will take diligence, determination, and discipline. Yet for the family willing to make a strong commitment and work together, it is achievable.

Study Questions

1. Have you ever been tempted to compromise a Scriptural principle due to a financial situation you found yourself in?

2. What Scriptural principles do we violate when we force a credit company to reduce our debt? Can you think of verses that support these principles?

3. Why is it so important to know the length of a loan?

4. Since inability to repay debt can provide a strong temptation to violate Scriptural principles, why would we get into any kind of debt to begin with? Are there certain kinds of debt that you feel are acceptable?

5. What is a key word often used in debt reduction advertisements that should alert you to a scam? Why should this word alert you?

CHAPTER TWELVE
Overcoming the Animal

A little child in Florida is strangled by a python her parents had in the house as a pet. A woman lies in the hospital in a coma, her face and hands mutilated by a pet chimpanzee. A nine-year-old girl is dead after being attacked by her stepfather's pet tiger.[8]

These newspaper headlines have shocked Americans in the last few years. Thousands of people in the United States each year are bitten, killed, and mauled by exotic pets. Many of us read these accounts in disbelief. Who would be so foolish as to buy a python and keep it in the house with small children? Why would someone keep a tiger in his home?

But the fact is that many people succumb to the temptation to purchase exotic animals such as monkeys, snakes, macaws, and even lions, bears, and tigers. As strange as it may sound, there are tigers and lions living in basements, monkeys sporting diapers, and alligators wearing leashes.

It should come as no surprise, then, that casualties occur. This should not be hard for people to understand. If you choose to bring a bear into your home, you have greatly increased your risk of being attacked by a bear. When you decide to share your home with a tiger, you are taking a chance. Tigers eat meat, and humans are a walking meal. So why do people do it? Why would you bring a lion into your home?

There may be differing answers to this question, but one reason people do not fear these animals is because of the size of the animal at the time of purchase. Most people do not go out and buy a two-hundred-pound tiger; they usually purchase small, cute cubs. Little thought is given to the fact that tigers, pythons, and bears grow up. Day after day, almost unnoticed by the owner, the charming little plaything changes into a fearful creature with dangerous claws and razor-sharp teeth. The cuddly darling has become a powerful animal capable of terrible destruction.

From Cute to King

Consumer debt has worked the same way in many of our homes. It came in the door as a little, harmless friend, promising to be a help and offering to enhance life and bring joy to the home. But seemingly overnight it has grown into a fearful animal capable of horrific destruction. We are not sure what to do with this beast that has no interest in leaving through the door it came in. It now fills the home with fear instead of the peace and tranquility it promised. We can't sleep at night, and worry keeps us from enjoying the day. We are suddenly brought to the shocking realization that things have changed. The friendly credit card has evolved from cute to king.

> ## The friendly credit card has evolved from cute to king.

What should a man do when he wakes up to find a man-eating tiger pacing up and down the hallway of his home? What should we do when we find that consumer debt is a beast within our home, threatening to devour us? In this chapter we want to look at some steps you can take to send the monster back out the door. Earlier we addressed the reality that dealing with consumer debt will not be easy, but this does not mean the monster cannot be defeated. After cowering in fear for years, many have finally annihilated the monster, and so can you! Let's look at some definite steps that can be taken.

- **Admit you have a problem.** If we fail to confess we have a problem with spending, it will be difficult to deal with debt. It is tempting to assume that next month will be better. Remember, time is important! Waiting to see what happens will only add to your debt.

- **Stop feeding the animal.** One of the first steps to slaying consumer debt is to stop feeding it. You will have to get serious with this if you are to be successful, and you may have to take drastic steps to achieve results. It may mean cutting up

all your cards or giving them to someone else for accountability, but you will not get out of debt while continuing to
take on more. If you are going to get out of the hole, you
must stop digging.

- **Size up the enemy.** This is extremely important. Make a list
  of all your debts so you know what you are fighting. Write
  down the loan amount, rate of interest, and the minimum
  that is due each month. Be diligent in this and make sure you
  leave nothing out. Include car loans and credit card debt, as
  well as any personal debt you have incurred. This will help
  you know where you stand and help you make informed
  decisions in the battle.

- **Communicate with creditors.** If individuals or institutions
  have extended credit to you, the least you can do is pick
  up the phone when you're in trouble. Creditors tend to get
  serious when a borrower goes silent. Don't be afraid to ask
  for a lower interest rate or different terms if you are having
  trouble making payments. Most creditors, including relatives you have borrowed from, are willing to work with you
  if they sense in you a desire to work with them. It is also very
  important to communicate with your spouse and family. A
  willingness to confess failure before them will help you fight
  more effectively. Family can be an invaluable tool in providing accountability, and your situation can help teach your
  family the importance of Biblical stewardship.

- **Pay off the smallest loans first.** As you look at your list of
  debts, pick out the smallest loan you have and put every extra penny on that debt. If all your consumer loans are close
  to the same amount, focus on the debts with the highest
  interest rates. But if you have some smaller debts that can be
  paid off quickly, you will then have more money available
  each month to put on the larger loans. This process is known
  as building momentum, or snowballing. Winning these first
  battles is a wonderful psychological boost. Discouragement
  is a great enemy in this process, and you will need these small

victories to keep you going. The monster of debt can be defeated, and these victories will give you courage to fight on.

- **Get help.** It is much easier to fight an enemy if you have a seasoned warrior by your side. Spend time in prayer over this, and the Lord may bring to mind someone in your congregation or community with whom you can share your battle. If you need additional assistance or have questions regarding how to proceed, there is help. Christian Aid Ministries has a Biblical Stewardship Services department that can provide assistance. To contact a staff member, write to kingdomfinance@camoh.org or call 330-893-2428.

- **Keep taking small bites.** How do you eat an elephant? One bite at a time. The same is true of conquering consumer debt. It probably did not grow to its current size in one month, and it will most likely not go away overnight. But if your family can unite against this giant and patiently continue to fight, you will experience victory. You can plot out a plan on paper and sit down occasionally to check progress. This can be an event that blesses your whole family.

Conclusion

If an individual is willing to apply himself to overcoming consumer debt, he can take helpful steps. In some situations, however, the individual seems unable or unwilling to make the needed changes to succeed. It then becomes the local church's responsibility to step in. This is not easy for the family in trouble, the local church, or those selected to help. Individuals chosen to help must have patience, yet be able to speak the truth in love. Time is important when dealing with consumer debt, yet much charity must be exercised. May the Lord give us wisdom as we endeavor to apply the words of the Apostle Paul: "Brethren, if a man be overtaken in a fault, ye which are spiritual, restore such an one in the spirit of meekness; considering thyself, lest thou also be tempted. Bear ye one another's burdens, and so fulfil the law of Christ."[a]

[a]Galatians 6:1-2

Study Questions

1. Why is it best to pay the smallest loans off first? Are there exceptions to this?

2. Discuss the best way for churches to deal with consumer debt when there is a problem. Has your congregation ever discussed this issue? Is giving money to the individual helpful?

3. Do you have periodic teaching on finances in your congregation? Why is this so vital in our culture?

4. Why is it so important to ask for personal accountability when struggling with consumer debt? Would individuals in your congregation be comfortable asking for it? Why or why not?

5. Why did Jesus spend so much time talking about finance? What should we learn from this?

CHAPTER THIRTEEN
The Vaccine

We all enjoy reading the history of new inventions and discoveries. The fascinating lives of men like Thomas Edison, Henry Ford, or the Wright brothers captivate us. These men kept pursuing their ideas until they invented things that changed millions of lives. They could look into the future and see possibilities their peers couldn't see.

But perhaps the stories that have made the most lasting impressions on me are accounts of men who have made great medical discoveries and invented life-changing cures. Today we hardly understand what it would have been like to live without antibiotics or with the fear of bubonic plague. Men argue over what the most important medical discovery might have been. Some feel it is penicillin, and others talk of various vaccines, but my guess is that the most significant discovery is the one that directly affected your own family. I can only imagine the excitement of finding out someone has discovered a cure for your illness. Imagine the thrill of being immunized against a disease that has ravaged humanity for centuries. One little injection, and fear of that disease is suddenly gone!

The history of smallpox is a good example. For centuries this sickness plagued humanity. An estimated seven million people died in the early days of the Roman Empire, and several major epidemics occurred during the Middle Ages. Millions lived in fear of finding the small spots on their skin. People tried a variety of cures, to no avail. Some tried herbal remedies, and others argued that draping special clothes over the infected areas would help. Some doctors believed bedroom windows should always be left open, and others told their patients to never have an open fire in the room. But in spite of all the precautions, men, women, and children continued to die.

Late in the eighteenth century, Edward Jenner began working on what finally became the first successful vaccine for smallpox. Imagine how it felt to receive this vaccine and finally be free from this dreadful plague. Just one injection of this substance into your bloodstream, and fear was gone. No longer did they need to look closely at their skin each morning. They were liberated from the dark, oppressive cloud of smallpox.

The Plague of Consumer Debt

Consumer debt has some strong similarities to the plague of smallpox. Like smallpox, it is an infectious disease. It has rolled like a wave across our society, infecting every level. From our national and local governments to our businesses and families, no segment is untouched. Our forefathers knew little of it, but in our day consumer debt has spread like an epidemic and threatens to destroy us. The average American home has succumbed to this scourge, and our churches are not immune. Is there no hope for our young families? Does it have to be like this? Is there a cure for this plague?

There is.

The Vaccine

Amazingly enough, the cure has been available for thousands of years. Consumer debt in our day is being cunningly marketed in an infinite number of new ways, but it is still designed specifically for an age-old problem. Though it can be devious and devastating and has brought many a man to ruin, only one type of person is susceptible to its infection.

As powerful as this mighty virus of consumer debt is, only the discontent are vulnerable. Consumer debt rarely has any power over the man who has contentment flowing through his veins. But the man

> **As powerful as this mighty virus of consumer debt is, only the discontent are vulnerable.**

who attempts to battle the endless onslaught of consumer marketing today with a discontented heart is wide open for infection.

We live in a discontented age. There has never been a time when so much has been available. No matter what your interest or hobby is, there are endless items to fill your cravings, and credit is available so you can have it now. So why are we discontent? Why does our generation seem unable to simply enjoy the blessings that surround us? Why are we always pursuing more?

Tough Times

My mother grew up in the small farming community of Sawyer, Kansas, back in the thirties. Times were difficult during those years, and those who lived through that time have many stories to tell. I grew up hearing stories about her family saving to make the $75 mortgage payment at the end of each year. She told stories of hoeing the corn by hand, killing chickens for dinner, and shoveling twenty-one wagonloads of sand out of the creek bed as a small child to help her father make concrete. Money was so scarce that my mother remembers hearing her father say on a Monday morning, "There is just enough gas in the car to go to church next Sunday, so we will not be able to drive anywhere this week."

They weren't concerned about fashion, trends, or name-brand products. In their home, receiving used shoes was cause for great rejoicing, even if they didn't fit very well. Working all day was normal, and their goal was survival. One of my mother's favorite stories was about the time she and her sisters were rewarded for a year of faithful work in the cornfield. They were so excited! There were few gifts given during that time, and I could still see the thrill in her eye as she remembered. To reward them for their diligence, their father gave them each a special present—a brand new hoe.

Growing up, I listened to these accounts and struggled to understand. There was a huge gap between Mother's life in the wilds of Kansas and my own existence. I couldn't relate to that level of poverty and wasn't sure I wanted to. This was partly due to the fact that I tended to remember these stories at the most inopportune times.

We had quite a few walnut trees around our house when I was a boy, and it was my responsibility to hoe the weeds around them. The hot California sun beating down in the middle of the summer quickly dissipated any enthusiasm I might have originally had for the job, and I would find myself frequently heading to the house for another drink. It was easy to dwell on the unfairness of it all. Hoeing was hard. Thoughts like, "Why couldn't Daddy just spray these weeds?" would circle in my mind, and I suspected he was just trying to keep me busy. So back to the house I would trudge, remembering uncomfortably how hard my mother had worked as a child and how much she had enjoyed it.

To this lad, life seemed hard and work a nuisance. My mother, though living in the same home, had a completely different perspective. She could look out the window and see fresh peaches, walnuts, and grapes. From her viewpoint, this was a land of plenty and ease. She now bought her chicken at the store and had enough canned fruit in the storeroom to take her well into the next year. Admittedly, the fact that my mother and I were at different ages affected our perspectives, but there was something else. We had different expectations from life.

Expectations

This illustration is not intended to be a lesson on raising children. It is difficult to replicate the blessing of poverty. Many of us have tried to keep our children busy with projects, animals, etc. But it doesn't take a child long to figure out whether the projects are needed for survival or are being given to keep him out of mischief.

But perhaps this scene does provide an example of our problem with contentment today. My mother grew up with low expectations. When she got out of bed early in the morning, her options were few and she expected little. But when I started the day, my options were many and expectations high. There were places to explore, a bike to ride, things to build, and toys to play with.

My mother grew up viewing each day as a time one worked to survive. Play happened occasionally and was exciting. I viewed each day as a time to play. Work was a problem that cut into playtime. We grew up with different expectations.

Those of us who have been raised in prosperity are at a disadvantage in this fight against discontentment. We have high expectations. Few growing up in America today know what true poverty is. With few exceptions, our children are growing up with high expectations. We can't control where or when we were raised, so how are we to live a contented life today? What steps can we take that will bless us and our children? How can we inject ourselves with contentment and immunize ourselves against the viruses of materialism and consumer debt? Let's look at a few ways we can fight against the cultural pressure that threatens to engulf us.

- Resolve to live solely for the Kingdom of Jesus Christ. We discussed this earlier, but it needs to be repeated. Jesus gave an illustration of a man who found one pearl of great price. He was so excited that he sold everything he owned just to have this one pearl. The man who has no other desire than to know Jesus, live out His teachings, and help build His Kingdom will be a contented man. When a man gives up this life, he is expecting nothing from it. This truth is so simple, yet behind every discontented professing believer is a heart that has not fully surrendered.

  This Kingdom-building focus will affect every area of our lives. Jesus began one of His parables by saying, "Behold, a sower went forth to sow." Notice, the planting that occurred that day wasn't by accident. It didn't happen by chance. It was an intentional activity and his overriding goal. He did other things that day. He probably got dressed, ate his breakfast, loaded his bag with seed, and walked out to the field; but all the time he was doing these things, he had an ultimate goal in the back of his mind. His goal was to sow. Kingdom building is the same. It must be an intentional pursuit, and as it builds in our hearts, it will crowd out the desire for other things.

- Find simple and service-oriented ways to vacation and spend time with family. It is a blessing when families can be involved in activities together. There are many things families can do together that bless others and cost very little. We can help neighbors, assist disaster projects, and reach out to shut-ins in the community. Children can grow up learning to be of service and find fulfillment in serving others instead of themselves. These types of activities tend to be inexpensive as well.

I know one family who was not financially able to travel, so they decided to take imaginary trips. In the evening they would get out the encyclopedia and various travel guides from the library and make their way through different states and countries. They would discuss the facts of each area as they went, and their children grew up with a much better understanding of geography and culture than many children who have spent much time traveling.

- Acquaint your family with the living conditions in other parts of the world. Many publications and newsletters can help keep you aware of living conditions around the world and give you a different point of reference. As your family discusses the harshness of life in Africa, for example, living room carpet showing definite signs of wear doesn't look quite as bad. Discussions around the dinner table regarding ways we can assist believers under persecution will take your focus off the "need" for new kitchen cabinets. Using something besides materialistic America as a point of reference will have a powerful influence on your list of needs.

- Avoid using advertisements for recreational reading. If your family sits around in the evening and gazes longingly at all the catalogs, flyers, and brochures that come into your home, you will build discontentment. I encourage people to open mail by the trash can and immediately dispose of unneeded advertisements. If you think you may need catalogs later, find an inconspicuous place to keep them. If you leave them lying around, you invite discontentment.

- Purpose to fill your home with thanksgiving. The psalmist David said that men who follow God "shall abundantly utter the memory of thy great goodness, and shall sing of thy righteousness."[a] Most of us can think of homes where thanksgiving seems to just pour out of every crack, where spontaneous singing and laughter float out of each window regardless of circumstances. We are all made up differently, and while a few seem grateful by nature, most of us have to choose to be thankful. It must not have come easy for the Apostle Paul either. While held captive for his faith in Rome, he wrote these words: "for I have learned, in whatsoever state I am, therewith to be content."[b]

Conclusion

The greatest vaccine available against the scourge of consumer debt that is plaguing our society is contentment. Paul told Timothy, "But godliness with contentment is great gain."[c] Not only will a home that pursues godly contentment avoid consumer debt, they will also save themselves from a myriad of other distressing concerns. Worry, covetousness, fear, and temptations can also be avoided. Paul continues to list the many problems the discontented man will encounter. Tremendous blessing is available to the man who will pursue contentment in God. Paul summarizes his message by saying, "And having food and raiment let us be therewith content."[d] Contentment not only sounds simple—it is!

[a]Psalm 145:7
[b]Philippians 4:11
[c]1 Timothy 6:6
[d]1 Timothy 6:8

Study Questions

1. Are you a contented person? Would your family agree? How about your co-workers?

2. How will focusing on the Kingdom affect our financial life?

3. Is building the Kingdom the most important personal goal in your life? Would your family agree?

4. Why is it so important to use something other than materialistic America as a reference point in our lives? What kind of reading material increases contentment in a home? What kind destroys it?

5. What kinds of activities can serve as recreation and Kingdom building at the same time?

Part Four
Where Are We Going?

CHAPTER FOURTEEN
Working as a Unit

In the preceding chapters we looked at the importance of taking steps to find out where we are financially and at the danger of going down the road of consumer debt. The next step is deciding where we want to go, and then we will plot a course to our goal. As we begin this section, it is important to first address the need for working as a family unit. If a husband and wife are not united on where they want to end up, there will be confusion in the home. Every little decision will create another battle, and the marriage, family, and witness of the home in the community will be destroyed. Many misunderstandings and hard feelings have resulted simply because a husband and wife were attempting to reach different goals. Let's begin by looking at the importance of a united vision and a home in the Bible that portrays this.

A Woman With a Vision

It was a dark time in Israel. There had been a string of ungodly kings, bloody wars, and a time of drought and famine. But right in the middle of this dismal scene, the Bible tells about a certain woman who was able to see more than just the surrounding gloom. The Bible says she was a great woman. From the account it is evident she was a believer in hospitality and had a greater level of perception than the other women of her day. She lived in Shunem, and we refer to her today as the Shunamite woman.

The prophet Elisha traveled through this village frequently, and the Bible says that as he made his way through, this woman would constrain him to stop and eat. She applied some pressure on Elisha.

As time went on, this woman developed a vision and began relaying this idea to her husband. She told him she perceived this was a holy man of God, and then she suggested, "Let us make a little chamber, I pray thee, on the wall; and let us set for him there a bed, and a table, and a stool, and a candlestick: and it shall be, when he cometh to us, that he shall turn in thither."[a]

The account goes on to tell how this husband and wife followed through with this vision and how the Lord blessed their home because of their faith in God and their care for Elisha. But the message we want to glean from the example of the Shunamite woman is the manner in which she pursued her vision.

Very little is said about the husband in this account. It seems that the woman in this story was more perceptive and visionary than her husband. She is the main player in the story. She is the one who went out and invited Elisha in, recognizing this wasn't just an ordinary man. It was the wife who produced the initiative and idea. But the husband had an important role, and there are two lessons we want to learn from this account.

- The wife did not implement the vision without her husband. Even though the idea and vision were hers, she communicated with her husband first. Notice the respectful way she spoke to him. She used the words "I pray thee," giving us to understand this was a request rather than a command. Each of us is made up differently, and many times women are more perceptive. We can all think of homes where the wife is more inclined to invite company and show hospitality and where she is more outgoing and disposed toward reaching out to the neighbors. But God honors the wife who reverences and gives preference to her husband.

- The husband had a good attitude about it. Most husbands have trouble playing second fiddle. Furthermore, many of us are married to wives who can play many fiddles bet-

---

[a]2 Kings 4:10

ter than we. We want to lead, and sometimes we fail to respond with grace to our wives' suggestions. But a wise husband is sensitive to his wife's intuition, and this husband was evidently humble enough to recognize his wife's God-given gifts.

In this account I see a man who knew from past experience that his wife had abilities he didn't. She was able to perceive things he hadn't considered and could see events from a better viewpoint. Rather than letting this frustrate and anger him, he evidently accepted this and supported his wife's vision. He considered the facts and embraced her vision, and together they began building the room for Elisha. This account is not intended to teach that the wife should be the leader and will always have proper vision. But this account does illustrate the beauty and blessing of a couple working together as a unit.

Uniting on Vision

If your home is going to be successful in pursuing Biblical stewardship, you will need to unite on where you are going. We have been raised in different homes. Some of us came from homes where little thought was given to finance. There was always plenty of money available, and when an item was needed, it was purchased. Others have grown up in settings where money was talked about constantly. Finances were tight, and there was never quite enough to buy necessities.

Some homes view money as a private matter, and because of this, children never hear the topic discussed. Other homes make many decisions by group consensus, and the children are included in the process. Because of the diversity in our homes on how finances are dealt with, many times we enter marriage with different expectations. A young woman raised in an affluent setting who marries a young man who has been raised frugally may be shocked and hurt when she returns home from her first grocery shopping experience and is questioned about the price she paid for the hamburger. These issues are real in new relationships, and if little discussion has occurred before the wedding, it is almost inevitable that problems will occur.

But without a united vision, disagreements will continue long after the first few years. I know of situations in which, after many years, the topic of finance is still very painful. The husband cannot understand why his wife spends so much on clothes, and she can't comprehend why he gets upset about a $50 pair of shoes, yet is willing to spend $900 on an boat motor he will probably only use twice a year. This type of friction will never end until a couple is willing to agree upon and share a united vision.

On the other hand I know of couples who, long before their wedding day, committed their finances to the Lord and purposed to walk together toward a common goal. They continue to talk about their larger vision, and they weigh every little decision that comes along in light of their greater vision. One brother I have come to appreciate had a conviction, as a young man, to live simply. He wanted to pursue a service-oriented occupation that he knew would bring in little income. So, while courting his prospective bride, he brought this topic up. He shared his vision with her and let her know he would probably never have enough money to purchase his own home. She had grown up in a nice home, and some of this was new to her. But they discussed it, she prayed about it, and eventually she embraced his vision. Their home continues to be a blessing to many as they pursue a united vision.

I am also painfully aware of another marriage where the husband has always had a vision of a home where the Lord Jesus is exalted by every decision, therefore wanting his family to consume as little as possible in order to share freely with those in need. This husband is married to a wife who, though she likes her husband's vision, doesn't embrace it fully. She wants a Christ-centered home, but she is afraid of being despised by other young mothers in her congregation. Even though she appreciates her husband's vision, she tends to be driven by her fears. When it is time to purchase clothing for the children, she buys name-brand clothing even though it is not consistent with her husband's vision. When it is time to prepare for company, she tends to buy extravagant groceries simply because she wants to be accepted.

Regrettably, this happens far too frequently in our Plain congregations. In the situation above, the husband is not at the grocery store when food is bought and does not know the differences in clothing prices. Consequently, he does not realize how much of a drain this is on their budget and why they do not seem to be able to help others as much as they would like.

Communication

It is impossible to overemphasize the importance of communication when discussing a united vision. I have often marveled at how little discussion takes place in many homes regarding financial goals. In most homes both the husband and wife are involved in spending money. This means they both are moving the home toward one goal or another, and if they are not united, confusion results.

Picture a young couple walking up to a pond. Seeing a rowboat tethered to the dock, they begin discussing how fun it would be to take a ride in the boat. The boat appears to be seaworthy, so with great enthusiasm they get into the boat, each one grabs an oar, and they begin rowing with zeal. Now let's suppose no discussion has occurred regarding where they plan to go. In their enthusiasm to get into the boat and on the water, no thought has been given to their final destination. Unknown to the young lady, the young man has his eye on a dock directly across the pond. As he rows, he envisions them pulling up smoothly beside the dock, tying up the boat, and then going for a stroll along

the bank. This vision has been clear to the man from the beginning, and though he hasn't told her, it is actually why he got into the boat.

The young woman, on the other hand, has a totally different picture in her mind. She pictures rowing along the shoreline, staying close to the bank, enjoying the trees and birds along the water's edge. So each of them, rowing on opposite sides of the boat, begin to pursue their vision. With every stroke of his oar, the young man attempts to point the bow of the boat toward the dock on the opposite shore, while the young woman continues to eye the shoreline and with a firm jaw pulls hard to bring the boat parallel with the trees along the water's edge.

Now how long do you suppose this scenario on the pond would play out without any discussion? And assuming there is no dialogue, what would happen? If there is no communication and no uniting of purpose, you know what will happen. They will expend much energy but probably won't reach either goal!

Sharing a united vision is a simple principle that is easy to understand when discussing rowboats. Somehow it is more difficult to comprehend with checkbooks. But the fact is that couples who continue to spend without uniting on vision will usually fail to reach meaningful goals.

Sharing the Vision With Children

Some parents shy away from discussing their financial vision with their children. Admittedly, if it is not done correctly, it can have negative effects. I know a man who grew up hearing his father constantly tell the family they were going broke. His father used this frightening message as a tool to reduce spending in the home. This man grew up under a cloud of continual fear and resolved he would never do this to his children. Sharing in order to manipulate should be avoided. Children should grow up with confidence, knowing their parents are trusting in God and His ability to provide.

But I believe the parents' vision should be communicated with the children, and if we fail to do so, we are missing a tremendous opportunity. Some families hold a family meeting periodically to help decide which charitable endeavor to help. It is important that parents agree on what level of openness to have with children. If the parents' vision is open and shared with the children, it will be much easier for them to understand why certain choices are made. Children will be less inclined, for example, to keep asking for unnecessary items if they understand the family's vision is to share as much as possible with those in poverty. It is a wonderful opportunity to prepare your children for survival in a materialistic society.

Children can also be instrumental in keeping a vision on track. I remember driving down the road years ago on my way to acquire some recreational equipment. It was something I had wrestled with and finally decided to go ahead and purchase. As we drove along, a question came from my son in the back seat. "Daddy, do you really think this is how God wants us to spend His money?" We can justify just about anything, and we have the ability to drift from our own teaching. But children have a way of seeing the world in black and white. They can be a powerful influence for good as we pursue a godly vision with our finances.

Study Questions

1. Why is it so important for a husband and wife to agree on where they want to go? If they fail to do this, what types of decisions will be difficult to make? Give some examples.

2. What lessons can we learn from the account of the Shunamite woman?

3. Why is it important for children to be included in some financial discussions in the home?

4. How much openness should we have with our children? Does telling our children about our giving conflict with Matthew 6:1-4?

5. Share ways in which your children have helped you with accountability.

Chapter Fifteen
An Overriding Vision

As we look at the importance of having an overriding vision, consider a man I met recently. To the average American observer, this man's life doesn't hold much attraction. With a low-paying job, seven children, and an extremely tight budget each month, there is little here to envy. He has no retirement account, little savings, and buys clothes for his family at the local thrift store. Here he is, living right in the middle of one of the most prosperous countries in the world, yet failing to make use of the opportunity that surrounds him. He is intelligent, educated, and in good health. With no accident or misfortune to blame, we could easily conclude his level of living is simply a result of poor financial planning.

Something must be wrong. You can tell just by looking. The rust spots peeking out through the faded paint on his old car confirm our suspicions about his ability to plan ahead. He's an American failure, as we can learn by further inquiry. We find he was recently offered another job that would have increased his income dramatically, but he turned it down. He said he likes the job he has and doesn't want to change. In fact, he is planning on spending even less time at work each week, which will further decrease his income. He admits things are going to be really tight, but he wants to spend more time doing other things. Who is this man? Does he lack vision?

Most people living in materialistic America today would agree: this man is a financial loser. But before you draw too firm a conclusion about him, let's look closer. It is true; he may never own his own home or travel beyond the adjoining state. He will probably never have a new car, and if he continues to follow his current path, he will not be able to retire with a guaranteed income. He certainly won't be able to sit back in his recliner in his older years and tell about the great financial moves he made.

Does all this speak of failure to you? Be honest. If this were a description of your son, would you be pleased? Obviously there is more to this story, so let me continue. Let me first say that I view this father as one of many Kingdom builders who are emerging out of our Anabaptist circles. He is a bright light shining out of materialistic America today. May the Lord raise up many more!

An Overriding Vision

This man is a minister in an Anabaptist church. He has made some choices that may seem absurd simply because he has a different vision than the surrounding society. His overall goal in life is to build the Kingdom of Jesus Christ, and his choices have been made to align with this overall Kingdom vision.

Let me explain further. His current occupation, while not producing much income, is helping to build the Kingdom. The older vehicles, used clothing, and lack of savings or a retirement program are simply part of the cost of this decision.

But why would he start working fewer hours each week? He was recently chosen for a position of leadership within his congregation, and as he looked about within his church, he became aware of a great need among the young men. This man and his wife spent time in prayer over this concern and decided the best way to address this need was for him to start spending more time with these struggling youth. This has been a difficult decision. It will place an additional strain on his wife as she attempts to stretch the budget even further, but both of them are committed to the Kingdom. They believe he has been called to be a shepherd, not just a sheepherder, and this seems to be the path the Lord is asking them to take. This young leader and his wife have an overriding Kingdom vision and are attempting to make sure every other decision, no matter how small, lines up with their greater goal.

The lesson from this account is not that each of us should be employed in a certain occupation, or that all of us should drive a certain model vehicle. I can think of other brothers who are pursuing a Kingdom-building vision, yet their lives do not look exactly like the story above. But here is a lesson not to be missed. Each of us has a vision, and your vision has a powerful influence on your life and what it produces. Stop here for a moment and do an analysis. What is the overriding vision of your life? Have you ever sat down and written it out? Is it possible that your financial problems are a result of an improper vision?

What Is Your Overriding Vision?

This topic of vision may seem pointless to you. Perhaps it seems like a waste of time to analyze your vision when what you really need is just more money in the checkbook. But I have found that our financial struggles are often a direct result of our overriding vision. All of us have many goals in life. Maybe it is difficult for you to identify an overriding goal, but I would propose you have one. As you examine your vision, be completely honest.

It is tempting just to say, "My ultimate goal in life is to bring glory to God." This sounds like a good vision, and such a statement would sound nice while sitting around with a group of church members studying the Word. But are the little choices you make each day proclaiming the same vision? Your vision will not be known as much by your stated goals as by the fruit of your life. Let's look at a few areas that can help us determine what our overriding vision really is.

- Jesus said, "For out of the abundance of the heart, the mouth speaketh."[a] If you really want to know the overriding vision of your heart, examine your words. What do you enjoy talking about? What topic are you most comfortable discussing? If you were going to give a talk, what subject are you best prepared for? We are generally most comfortable discussing topics we have given thought to. I have overheard pilots spend a whole evening talking about different airplanes, runways, and flight experiences. They are able to do this because they have a great interest

---

[a]Matthew 12:34

in the topic and have spent lots of time thinking about it. Identify what you enjoy discussing, and it will give you a clue as to what your vision and goals are in life.

- What are you willing to sacrifice time for? Time is a precious commodity. Examining our use of it can help reveal our vision. I remember a time in my life when physical exercise consumed my thoughts. I looked for time to jog or lift weights. I was willing to give up just about any activity in order to work out. But behind this flurry of activity was a purpose. I had a burning desire, an overriding vision, to be physically fit. I wanted to be admired for my physical ability, and I was willing to sacrifice a great number of hours to pursue this goal. What do you sacrifice time for, and what does this tell you about your overriding vision?

- Where is your discretionary income going? Your checkbook speaks volumes about your vision in life. Jesus said, "For where your treasure is, there will your heart be also."[b] As we mentioned in chapter two, if you want to know where your heart is, take a close look at where your money has been going. I find this truth very challenging. I like to think my life is devoted to God and that every part of it has been laid on the altar, but sometimes my checkbook reveals a different story. If you are serious about examining the overriding vision that is driving your life, take a close look at where your discretionary income is going.

The Battle for Vision

I am convinced every man has an overriding vision. He may not have given much thought to what that vision is, but it nevertheless drives the choices he makes. But I am also persuaded that every man's vision is under attack. We can see this in the business world around us. A battle is raging, and your vision is the focal point of the fight.

[b]Matthew 6:21

Capturing your vision is the objective of marketing schemes and advertising agencies. Every car salesman knows that if he can get you to visualize driving his product, the rest is easy. Travel agencies understand that if they can get you to picture yourself walking down those white beaches in the ocean breeze surrounded by the sound of the surf and the cry of the seagull, it will be much easier to make the deal. This is why pictures are used so profusely in advertisements and why the combination of sight and sound are so effective in marketing.

Kingdom of Self
Nice Retirement, Cruises,
2nd Home, New Car,
Designer Clothing, RVs

Kingdom of God
Helping the Poor, Feeding
the Hungry, Reaching the Lost,
Helping Widows/Orphans

But the most important battle for your vision is going on in another realm. All through the Bible, the battle is fought for man's overriding vision as both God and Satan attempt to show man the advantages of serving them. Satan wades into the battle early in Genesis. He enters into dialogue with Eve in a deceptive attempt to show how great life could be if she would only listen to him. Eve listens to Satan. She

> **God and Satan both understand; if you capture a man's vision, you have captured the man.**

pictures how wonderful it could be to become like gods, to be wise, to have her eyes opened, and to taste that fruit.

All through the Bible this battle for vision continues until finally in Revelation the Lord gives suffering saints a picture of the magnificent glory to come. God and Satan both understand; if you capture a man's vision, you have captured the man. Believers throughout history have been sustained through great persecution and torture by

117

an overriding vision, a picture in their minds, of soon being with the Lord. Even the Lord Jesus Himself was sustained by a vision of "the joy that was set before him."

Conclusion

Our decision making in life is driven by our overriding vision. When a man's overriding vision changes, every part of his life is impacted. This truth is evident in the early church. Consider the dramatic change in the lives of those early believers immediately after they met the Lord. "And all that believed were together, and had all things common; And sold their possessions and goods, and parted them to all men, as every man had need."[c]

These words always amaze me. I picture men from all backgrounds and social levels sitting around a room. I see men worth five million dollars sitting next to others who don't have twenty dollars to their name. Two weeks ago this one fact placed them in different worlds. But now something has changed. Suddenly the man worth five million is willing to give it all up. He who had worked for this money, guarded it, and worried about losing it is suddenly giving it away. Amazing! Why would anyone do this?

Two weeks ago his life was about him. His overriding vision and goal was admiration from friends, ease of life, and security from fear or want. But he unexpectedly found all his needs met in this man called Jesus Christ. Suddenly all the things he had esteemed—wealth, security, and prestige—seemed worthless in light of what he had found. He had found something of such value that he wanted nothing in his life to distract from it. He had a position in a Kingdom and a relationship with a King that was worth far more than five million dollars. This overriding Kingdom-building vision is still available today, and it is encouraging to see many of our young families rising up to embrace it.

---

[c] Acts 2:44-45

Study Questions

1. Would you be content if your child chose a Kingdom-building path in life that never allowed him to own his own home? Would you be content if he drove to church in an older vehicle?

2. Can you share a time in your life when a financial difficulty was the result of an improper overriding vision?

3. Discuss some ways Satan is attempting to influence the vision of young families in your church. What about your youth?

4. How can the Lord use a proper vision to take us through difficulty? Can you think of times in the Bible when God gave His people a vision of the future to sustain them?

5. Discuss the sharing of goods within the early church. Does your congregation have this kind of love for the Lord and for each other? Is your passion for Jesus stronger than your focus on personal possessions?

Chapter Sixteen
Establishing a Vision for Discretionary Income

We have looked at the importance of having a godly financial vision and the necessity of uniting and discussing this vision as a family. Now we will look at how to develop and establish this overriding vision for our homes. It is not possible to describe a vision that will fit every person and circumstance. Each family will need to seek the face of God in this. All of us come from different backgrounds and have different gifts. The specifics of our vision will be tempered by our marriages, our church fellowships, and our own abilities. God will also call us, as believers in His body, to different roles. Paul is very clear about this in his letter to the church at Corinth. God has a special place for each person in the body. But God is calling all of us to have a vision for work within the Kingdom He is building.

In this chapter we want to stand back and consider an average life span to help us grasp a clearer vision for our individual lives. We want to specifically look at establishing a vision for discretionary income. As mentioned earlier, discretionary income refers to the funds we have left over after we have bought what is needed for survival.

Let's begin by considering a hypothetical life span of a couple living here in America. We will call them Jim and Jane. As we examine their life, you can follow the income and expense of their home on the graph on the following page.

The upper line on the chart (at the top of the black) represents the income Jim brought home, and the lower line (at the top of the gray) represents the expenses required to operate their home.

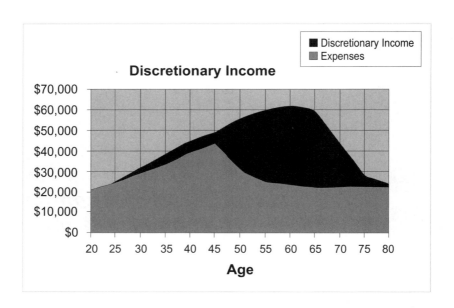

Discretionary Income

Legend: ■ Discretionary Income ■ Expenses

Jim's Income

As you can see by looking at the graph, Jim started his married life at the age of twenty with an annual salary of $21,000. At eighteen Jim had started working for one of the brothers in his congregation who owned a company we will call Reliable Plumbing. Jim did not have any previous experience in plumbing, but he learned fast. His income continued to climb. His employer appreciated his faithfulness and gradually gave him more responsibilities. By the time Jim was forty-five, his income had increased to almost $50,000 per year.

When Jim was fifty years old, there were some changes at Reliable Plumbing. Jim's employer needed to slow down due to health concerns, and Jim was asked to begin working in the office. As you can see on the graph, Jim was reimbursed for this change in his job description, and his income continued to climb. Finally, at the age of sixty, Jim asked the company if he could be relieved of some of his responsibilities. This reduced his income substantially, and by the time Jim was seventy-five years old, he was only working two days a week and earning $23,000 each year. Jim's health began to deteriorate at this point. For the next five years he continued working less, and then Jim and Jane both died at the age of eighty.

Jim's Expenses

As you can see from the bottom line on the graph, Jim's expenses also made some changes over the years. Those first few years were pretty tough. After all the necessary expenses were met, there wasn't much left over. Jane did the best she could, and after five years Jim and Jane were able to put a small down payment on an older farmhouse that needed some repairs. Over the next ten years, they had six children. Each of these children brought additional costs to the home. Finally, after being married for twenty-five years, some changes occurred that greatly affected their expenses. The year Jim turned forty-five they paid off their mortgage, and their oldest child married and left their home.

You can see on the chart that, for the first time in their married life, their expenses began to fall. Due to the house being paid off and children continuing to leave the home, Jim and Jane's expenses continued to fall. During the last ten years, their expenses remained relatively stable each year until they died.

Discretionary Income

Looking back over the lives of Jim and Jane, we can see how various changes affected both their income and expenses. Jim became more valuable to Reliable Plumbing as he gained experience, and he was reimbursed accordingly. Their expenses fluctuated as well. Expenses increased as the family grew, and then dropped dramatically as the mortgage was paid off and the children left home. But now we will leave the expenses and income and look at the area between the two. This area, which is black on the graph, represents the discretionary income throughout Jim and Jane's life. This is the money that flowed through their hands and was not needed to survive.

We want to use this chart in several ways, but before we begin, we need to realize that this graph will not address every situation. Some may earn much more than this, and some less. Your family may have special costs due to health issues, or you may have experienced a calamity of some kind.

Disregard the numbers as much as possible and try to grasp the overall principle. The goal of this chart is simply to help us get a picture of discretionary income and gain a vision for its proper use.

Seasons of Life

One of the first lessons we can gain from this chart is the fact that the average lifespan has seasons. Many young couples who are raising large families wish they could give more than they do. They read the newsletters that come into their homes from various charitable organizations and wish they were able to share more.

I believe everyone living in America today should be giving to those in need, but we also need to understand that life has seasons. As you look at the chart, it is obvious that Jim and Jane had much more money available during the last half of their lives than they did when they were first married. Worrying about the fact that we are not able to give as much as we would desire can be counterproductive. The result can be discouragement, and it can cause a young couple to feel unproductive in the Kingdom. Understand that our lives have seasons. Rather than always longing for the next season, enjoy and build the Kingdom where you are.

> **Rather than always longing for the next season, enjoy and build the Kingdom where you are.**

Early Years – Develop the Vision

Look over the graph of Jim and Jane's life again and notice those first years of marriage. Look specifically at the time between twenty and thirty years of age, and you will notice there is little discretionary income during those years. Because of this it is easy to assume those years are not very important to this study. But I firmly believe those years are the most important years on the graph. This is the time when most young families have little to give, yet something of profound importance is occurring. They are developing a vision.

The Leaning of Our Longings

Couples during this time in their marriage develop longings. The direction those longings lean will greatly influence the remainder of their lives and the lives of their children. Jim and Jane's graph shows us how much discretionary income was available during each part of their life, but it does not tell us how they chose to use it. Let's assume that during the first ten years of their married life they both focused on society and the affluence that surrounded them. They looked at the nicer homes other families had and observed the new vehicles being driven by those who could afford them. Even though they could not afford these things, they began to long for them.

Conversations in their home went something like this. "I wish we could afford a car like Fred just bought. And someday I would really like to redecorate our bathroom. Did you see how nice Sally's looks since they remodeled theirs?" If they had longings like this during their early years, what would have happened to Jim and Jane's extra money when the mortgage was finally paid off? The answer is obvious. Money tends to follow our longings, and without even having been aware of what was happening, the money that had been going to the mortgage would have begun flowing toward the things they had been longing for.

But imagine how different Jim and Jane's lives would have looked if during those early years they had focused on the Kingdom. Just suppose they had learned to view themselves as stewards and had purposed to use every resource God had given them to bless others. Imagine how conversations in their home might have gone. "I just heard that sister Sarah's car is in the shop again. I wish we had enough money to help her buy one that isn't always having trouble. And I just read there is a desperate need for Bibles in some of the countries where Christians are being persecuted. I wish there was some way we could send more to help them." Again, money tends to follow our longings eventually. If those early years in Jim and Jane's home had been spent focusing on the Kingdom, what would have happened? Every spare dollar would have been directed toward the needs of others, and as more money became available in their older years, that money would also have tended to follow the longing they had developed.

Latter Years – Demonstrating the Vision

The Bible records the lives of men who had godly desires when they were young, but when they became older, their hearts were turned away from serving the Lord. We think of kings like Solomon and Asa. These men were sold out for God in their youth, yet in their older years they became distracted. Unfortunately, we observe the same drift all too often in our churches. At first we see young men with a passion for serving the Lord, raising up godly seed, and sharing the Gospel. But sometimes it seems they slowly lose their fire. They give up their fire for the Kingdom and exchange it for recreation, travel, and hobbies. They found it easy to talk about the inconsistency of buying a second home back when they couldn't afford one anyway, but when they got older and money became more plentiful, they began to look at things differently. Suddenly it was easy to justify things they were once opposed to.

As you look at the graph of Jim and Jane's life, it is obvious that most of their discretionary income was available to them between the ages of fifty and seventy. This is true in most homes here in America. If you have a godly vision, these years can be a time of wonderful blessing and opportunity. Those of us in this stage of life can greatly encourage young families who are watching. This is your time to demonstrate a Kingdom vision.

Those who are younger and are struggling financially need encouragement in the midst of the weekly grind, and the older generation has the power to encourage or discourage them. Young fathers go to church each week and listen to messages on the blessing of surrendering all to Jesus. They hear good teaching on Biblical separation from the world and how it affects every decision of their lives. But they become discouraged as they watch the older generation pour their resources into leisure, hobbies, and home improvement.

But I have also seen the opposite. As a young father I was encouraged to see older brethren who, although they had the means to pursue a path of relaxation, used their time and money to sort clothes for those in need, assist widows, and help rebuild after disasters. They demonstrated that there was more to life than just playing with grandchildren and seeking personal fulfillment. I can think of older believers who have filled their lives with writing letters of encouragement to those who are discouraged and making phone calls to support those who are weak. Their hours are filled doing the things they always longed to do when they were younger—strengthening and building the Kingdom!

I know of one sister living in a retirement center, well into her eighties, who uses her time speaking to others in the facility about the condition of their souls. She once commented to me, "These people in here need to hear about the Lord. Some of them don't have much more time to live!" These are the older soldiers in the Lord's army who inspire those who are younger. They are proving by their lives that what they verbally profess is true. They are demonstrating that the Kingdom of Jesus Christ is worth everything to them.

Conclusion

No matter where you are on the chart of life, it is not too late to establish a Kingdom vision. Take one more look at the graph that shows Jim and Jane's financial life. Suppose this is a picture of your life and you are at the end of your time here on earth. Imagine, for a moment, that all the black on the chart represents the discretionary money that has gone through your hands—the cash you controlled beyond the basic necessities.

When you are eighty, what will you wish this money had been used for? More important, how did God want His money to be used? Every steward will have a day to give account. How will God regard your stewardship? Let these questions motivate you in establishing a Christ-centered vision for your home. Your overriding vision for your finances is very important and will affect every part of your life. Take time to analyze it closely and prayerfully. Spread it out before the Lord.

It is also important that families write down their vision for financial stewardship. In the book of Habakkuk, the prophet was waiting for direction and a vision from the Lord. When a vision was finally given, God told Habakkuk, "Write the vision, and make it plain upon tables, that he may run that readeth it."[a] There is something about writing down our goals that helps us remember. If you are willing to develop and establish a godly financial vision for your life, you will not only find spiritual blessing, but you will also find relief from many of the financial difficulties that trouble our homes today.

Study Questions

1. Why is it important to understand that there are seasons in life? What can be the results of failing to understand this?

2. How can you encourage young couples in your congregation to develop godly longings? Are the pressures your young families feel encouraging them to build God's Kingdom or their own?

3. Why is it so important for older families to show by their example that they are living for the Kingdom?

4. When life is over, how will you wish your discretionary income had been used?

5. Discuss some examples of goals that might be included in an overriding vision.

[a]Habakkuk 2:2

CHAPTER SEVENTEEN
Establishing Goals

Before we discuss potential long-term goals, I think it is important to reiterate the importance of couples setting financial goals together. I believe the most effective way to discuss and establish a vision and long-term goals for your home is to take a day away from the house and children. You may not need a whole day, but take enough time to pray and discuss your situation together. Begin by discussing your overriding vision for your home. What is it? Are you both committed to using every resource at your disposal to build the Kingdom?

Be honest with each other. Are you struggling with other desires? Do you feel pressure from your social group or church family to live at a certain level? Are you fearful that surrendering your finances to the Lord might mean driving an older vehicle and bringing embarrassment to your family? These issues need to be discussed, and the more open you can be with each other, the more effective your home will be in the Kingdom. But it is also extremely important that you have charity for each other. These issues get very close to our hearts, and it is of utmost importance that you walk together.

Each of us is at a different place, and it will not be possible to cover all the potential goals each family might have. But let's look at a few financial goals you might consider for your home.

Debt-Free Living

Before discussing any other goals, it is important to address debt-free living. This goal should be at the top of your long-term goals, regardless of where your finances are or how you have been raised.

You may have already purposed to live debt-free and have convictions against debt of any kind. God bless you.

Or you may be struggling with debt and trying to find relief from its shackles. May the Lord bless you as well. If you are in this situation, your first goal should be to overcome the debt you have and establish a vision for long-term, debt-free living. Let's start by breaking debt down into three categories and looking at each type of debt separately.

- Consumer Debt—As you establish long-term goals, you need to understand the importance of breaking the cycle of consumer debt. In addition to credit cards, it is easy to fall into the trap of vehicle loans. We will discuss ways to break this cycle later, but first get a vision of living without payments. Payment-free living is a goal worth pursuing.

- House Loans—If you decide buying a home is for you and borrowing to achieve this is part of your Kingdom vision, I believe it is important to establish a vision for paying that loan off as soon as possible. Even though I would consider this type of debt different from credit card debt, it is important to understand that debt of any kind puts a shackle around us. It is difficult to

> **It is difficult to read the teachings of Jesus with an open heart while chained to Bank of America . . .**

read the teachings of Jesus with an open heart while chained to Bank of America, and we want nothing in our lives that will obscure our ability to hear the Word of the Lord.

- Business Loans—Our business culture today teaches us that businesses tend to be more profitable when using other people's money. In other words, a company can grow much faster and be more lucrative by borrowing. This is true in many situations. But we must ask ourselves another question if we are serious about Kingdom living. "Must every business decision be made in the light of profitability?" I am not saying there is never a time for a business to borrow. But there is a wonderful freedom in operating a business debt-free, and I would encourage business owners to make this their goal. Business debt has a way of encouraging ongoing business growth and subtly causing us to shift our focus toward business building rather than Kingdom building.

Wherever you are right now with regard to debt, take time to consider the blessing of debt-free living. The freedom that accompanies living without monthly payments is of great value. Make it a long-term goal for your home.

Purchasing a Home

One of the decisions that faces every couple is where they will live. Prevailing wisdom has been that, over the long term, purchasing a home is better and less expensive than renting one. Recently, however, many young couples are challenging this conclusion. They believe that ultimately more is spent in owning and that more money could be used for building the Kingdom if a family was willing to find simple housing for rent. Their logic is that a home becomes more than shelter to us, and a large amount of cash that could be used for the Kingdom gets used in such things as continual upkeep, home improvement, and landscaping. Leaving this debate aside, we can all agree we must live somewhere. Perhaps the greater question for us is, at what level are we going to live?

As you consider the long-term goal of whether or not to purchase a home, maybe you first need to ask yourself what your goal really is. As you look at your options, are you visualizing a shelter or a showplace? Regardless of what others around you are doing, take some time to prayerfully consider this question.

> **. . . are you visualizing a shelter or a showplace?**

We need to acknowledge that our homes have the capability of becoming much more than shelter. They become expressions of who we are and can be attempts to create little Edens here on earth. May the Lord give us the ability to examine ourselves in this area and grant us a heavy dose of charity as we observe the choices of others.

Before leaving this topic, I think it is only fair to say that historically here in the United States it has been better to purchase a home than to rent long-term. Inflation has greatly affected this, and though we have no way of knowing the future, we can only assume it will continue as it has in the past. All this should be discussed as you consider your financial goals, and perhaps purchasing a home will be part of your overriding vision. But regardless of your decision concerning buying versus renting, be sure you seek the Lord as you consider size and extravagance. Pray that the Lord would give you wisdom as you seek to create an environment that, while welcoming to the visitor, is not a continual cash-consuming display.

Hanging on the wall in my office is a picture of a widow who lives in Haiti. She is standing in front of a little mud hut wearing a pleasant smile and an old scarf for a head veiling. I met this woman in 2002 while visiting her hometown of Port-à-Piment. We stopped to visit her on a Sunday afternoon, and she graciously welcomed us into her little house. It didn't take long to see where she lived, since the whole house was about the size of a small bedroom. She was excited to share with visitors the many ways the Lord had blessed her. She spoke of how she had hoped someday she could have a metal roof, and after many years of praying, she had been able to purchase one just last year. Then, apparently realizing we were not as excited about her mud hut as she was, she made this final joyful observation regarding her life. "Look at me. I don't have many possessions, but I have Jesus, and that is all I really need!"

I looked around at the dirt floor, the single chair, and the small, rickety table. I looked up at the metal roof full of nail holes, obviously not sheltering its first home, and pondered, *Do I have this level of contentment with my home?*

When Father's Day came around, I opened a gift from my children and found a framed picture of this woman for my wall. Those who surround me know my weakness well! They knew I needed a constant reminder. I still look at that picture and ponder. I don't know where this woman is today, but her picture still speaks to me. It is so easy for our homes to become more than shelter. Wherever you live, take time to be thankful, and as you establish a vision for a house to live in, may the home you envision be a display of Kingdom living.

Preparing for Declining Years

Few topics have captured the American mind like retirement. Our mail, newspapers, and magazines are all full of ways to plan. All promote the same theme: "You are not saving enough for retirement." The advertisements go on to tell how their product or financial vehicle can take you where you want to go. Pictures show gray-haired, smiling people walking on beaches, touring Europe, or living in peaceful, gated retirement communities. The ads insinuate that you must act now if you want to be smiling later.

What is your vision for your declining years, and more important, what is God's vision? Before discussing whether or not you should be saving for this time in your life, I highly recommend some honest discussion between you and your spouse. Ignore society's recommendations and prayerfully consider how you can best continue building the Kingdom during these years. Continue discussing and refining this vision as the years go by. Have open discussions with others in your age group and encourage them toward a Kingdom vision as well. This will help you polish your vision as you continue to hold it up before the Lord.

Should saving for declining years be a financial goal in our lives? Does saving for this time violate the teaching of Jesus to not lay up treasures on earth?* There are legitimate reasons to set money aside for known expenses, and whether or not you choose to save for retirement years will require thought and prayer. This question is not easy, and none of us should rush to answer it. We all should closely examine our visions and goals for our declining years. I know individuals who have

---

*There are various views on this topic, and I do not believe there is a one-size-fits-all answer to this question. We all believe there are times to save money. I have never heard of individuals who believed Jesus' teaching on laying up treasures so literally that they objected to a farmer saving money for seed in anticipation of the next planting time. All of us are forced to look into the heart of what Jesus was saying. For example, Jesus also said, "Labour not for the meat which perisheth, but for that meat which endureth unto everlasting life" (John 6:27). The literal words here would teach that we shouldn't labor to eat. Perhaps in these passages the point is primarily how much greater the blessing of obtaining eternal treasure is than temporal treasure.

been actively involved in Kingdom-building activities for many years, and by their own admission, they wouldn't have been able to do this had they never set any money aside. They now use those investments to cover basic necessities while they devote their time to ministry. But we need to be extremely careful as we analyze our hearts in this area. I have observed far more frequently among us a tendency to view these "golden years" as a time just to enjoy ourselves. The focus seems to be on hobbies, recreational equipment, enjoying our families, and frivolous travel. There may be a place for saving, but I believe our motives must be examined closely.

Before we leave this topic of planning for declining years, I think it is important to look briefly at how we take care of the elderly within our families and churches. I was blessed to grow up in a home where my parents actively assisted my grandparents. There may be times when rest homes and retirement facilities can be a blessing. Some parents like to maintain their independence as long as possible. But I also believe our generation has lost a tremendous blessing by neglecting our aged.

> ... I also believe our generation has lost a tremendous blessing by neglecting our aged.

blessing by neglecting our aged. The cost of rest homes and retirement facilities continues to soar. If the church could again bring the aged into our homes, an amazing amount of money would be freed for the Kingdom. But even beyond the financial waste, we are missing wonderful opportunities when we fail to care for the elderly—opportunities to teach our children respect for the aged, to demonstrate the blessings of living out Scriptural principles, to give and receive love, and to benefit from the wisdom of another generation.

Conclusion

We have only addressed a few of the many potential financial goals that could be considered. Each of us is in a different situation, but it is vital that every family discuss where they are going. It is also important to examine each financial goal in the light of your overriding vision. If your vision is to use your home and finances to the glory of

God and His Kingdom, then it is essential to ask if this is true of each long-term goal as well. Once you have determined where you are and where you want to go, you are in a position to move on to the next question: How can I get from where I am to where I want to go?

Study Questions

1. Why is it so important for couples to be united when establishing financial goals?

2. What did Jesus mean when He told us not to lay up treasures? Why do our hearts seek easy explanations for this verse?

3. Is it possible to hold wealth without it affecting our hearts? What did Jesus mean when He said "where your treasure is, there will your heart be also"?

4. Why should debt-free living be a goal? How can debt affect how we hear the Word of God?

5. From a Kingdom perspective, what are the advantages and disadvantages of owning a home?

6. Does God intend for us to save for retirement? Is this a proper use of His money? Are there ways your congregation could do a better job of taking care of the aged?

Part Five

How Can We Get
There From Here?

CHAPTER EIGHTEEN
Budgets—Do We Really Need One?

I t is seven o'clock, and as a new day begins, the jobsite comes to life. Workers carrying hand tools and lunchboxes pass through gates in the security fence, and backhoes, man lifts, and welders roar to life. I have worked in commercial construction in the past and am always impressed with the amount of power and energy that can be concentrated in such a small space. The workspace never seems large enough. Trades seem to be working on top of each other, and someone standing back observing the roar and seeming confusion could conclude that little is actually being accomplished. Sometimes it looks like chaos.

But if you peer through the security fence, you will usually notice a little building over to the side known as the job shack. You will see men coming and going out of this little building, and if you go inside, you will observe something else. You will see burly men with bulging biceps and heavy tools clanging around their waists looking intently at a large sheet of paper. This paper covered with drawings is known as "the plan." The plan is just some writing on paper, but it is very important.

The plan provides focus for all the energy that pours onto the jobsite each day. But a plan is only effective if the workers allow themselves to be guided by it. A man on an excavator or an ironworker with a torch could totally destroy a jobsite in a day. A project is only successful if each worker follows the plan. Workers understand this. I have been amazed as I worked beside some of these men. Commercial workers can be a rough lot. Many of them don't like being told what to do by the government, their wives, or their bosses, but when they arrive on the

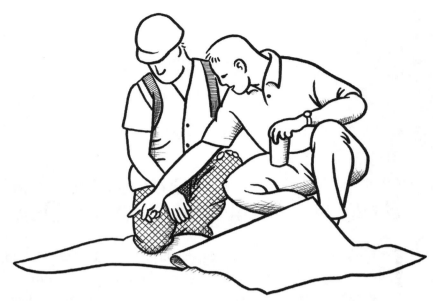

jobsite, they seem to understand the importance of following the plan.

As we think about using a budget, think about it like a plan on a jobsite. Just as jobsites need something to regulate the energy coming in the gates each morning, our homes need some regulation over the money that comes in. It seems men especially struggle to understand this. We understand the need for a plan on a jobsite, yet we react to having a piece of paper tell us whether or not we can make a purchase in our home. Somehow it seems like real men shouldn't need a budget.

Do Real Men Need a Budget?

Does everyone need a budget? Everyone needs some method of regulating finances. Perhaps you feel you are getting along fine. Budgets seem like a lot of unnecessary work in your situation. Maybe you have always viewed budgets

> **Everyone needs some method of regulating finances.**

as something for those who don't have the self-discipline to control themselves. Perhaps you are right. But I want to look at a few situations in which I believe a budgeting system is absolutely essential. Consider the following scenarios and see if you fit into any of them.

- A family carrying consumer debt. This would include credit cards, unsecured personal loans, or loans on vehicles. It is absolutely essential that we have controls on our spending and have a plan to reach our goals when attempting to pay off any type of consumer debt. Consumer debt is a sign that something isn't working.

- A family trying to reach a financial goal. Trying to reach a financial goal without a budget is like trying to construct a building without a plan. You need something to help you focus on the goal, and a properly crafted budget can do this for you.

- A marriage in which either husband or wife has a weakness for impulsive buying. Personalities are different, and many of us have that weakness. This means we go into a store with a list or with a particular item in mind and come out of the store with things we hadn't planned on buying. We will deal with this again later, but if this occasionally happens in your home, you need a budget.

- A family who is serious about Biblical stewardship. Some of us do not feel we need a budget because there is always enough money in the account to purchase what is needed. This may be because we have a very good income or because we are older and our expenses have diminished. Remember the life of Jim and Jane. Consider the last part of their lives and the large amount of money that was at their disposal. A budget is essential if you are serious about using this money for the Lord. A budget will assist you in directing more of your discretionary income into Kingdom building and less into self-centered activities.

- A couple who has experienced disagreements over finances. A budget can be a tremendous blessing in a marriage where misunderstandings and conflicts exist. A wife will feel much more confident when purchasing groceries if she knows she is within the agreed-upon budget. A husband will feel no guilt when buying that fishing rod he has had his eye on if he is using money they have set aside for recreation. A budget can help heal a marriage in which the use of money has been a source of contention.

If any of these scenarios describe your situation, I would highly recommend a budget for your home. Many of us have tried to pour gas into a small engine without a funnel. Picture gasoline in a five-gallon bucket and imagine attempting to pour it into a lawnmower. We have plenty of gas and a mower that needs it, but we need a way to control the gas and make sure it gets where it is needed.

This is the role of a budget. A budget is designed to put some restrictions on the flow of money from the checkbook. If too much money splashes around outside the target, we will never reach our goals. A budget does not need to be complicated, time-consuming, or bulky. A small funnel can achieve amazing results. But to be effective, a budget does need to be capable of providing some constraint on our spending.

Budgets Do Not Produce Miracles

One assumption many people have is that budgets somehow miraculously produce more money. Most people believe their problem is insufficient funds. If they just had more money, this would take care of their dilemmas. But in most homes insufficient income is not as great a problem as uncontrolled spending. Remember, the problem was not insufficient gasoline in the five-gallon bucket. The problem was that not enough gas was getting into the little hole. When people finally realize this truth, they will see the blessing in using a budget.

Conclusion

Successfully managing finances in a home is more difficult than most of us realized when we were first married. Most of us experienced some difficulty driving our personal financial vehicles before we were married, and after the wedding discovered that adding another steering wheel does not necessarily make a car easier to control. But even with two steering wheels and two people attempting to steer, we will be much more successful getting where we want to go if both drivers have a good road map and have agreed upon the destination and the route.

Study Questions

1. Discuss the difficulties you have had with budgets in the past. Have you found ways to overcome these struggles?

2. How can a budget help a family overcome consumer debt?

3. How can a budget help a couple when finances are putting a strain on their marriage? For this to be effective, why is it important for a couple to craft this budget together?

4. How can a budget help an older couple who has a desire to use their resources to bless the Kingdom?

5. How can a budget provide freedom in a marriage and help put an end to disagreements over small purchases?

Chapter Nineteen
Budgeting—Finding a System That Works

Ayoung man returned home to the family farm after graduating from college. After studying hard and receiving a degree in accounting, he couldn't wait to take a look at Dad's bookkeeping system. His father had been a hard-working man all his life and over the years had developed his own method of keeping track of finances. He hadn't been born in this country, and coming to America as a young man, all he had known was difficult times and hard work.

Upon arriving home, the son sat down at his father's desk and began looking over the books. The young man immediately realized his father's bookkeeping methods were completely outdated. His father had obviously been successful, but the young man could also see his father had no concept of the latest accounting techniques. He scanned the records in alarm and finally told his father, "Dad, you need some major changes here. With the way you keep books, how can you know whether or not you are making money?"

The farmer scratched his head thoughtfully and replied, "Son, you are probably right. I never had much education, and I am sure there are better ways to keep records. But son, I guess I figure a little like this. When I came to this country, I had two shirts, one pair of pants, and five dollars. Today I have two farms, a beautiful wife, five children, and some money in savings. As near as I can figure, if you take what I have and subtract the shirts, pants, and the five dollars, all the rest is profit."

Keep It Simple

Now it was probably true that the son had learned some good techniques from which his father could benefit. But it is also true that bookkeeping doesn't need to be complicated to work. This farmer had a method that worked for him. Many people believe a budgeting system needs to be complex and time-consuming to be effective. I believe the opposite is true. A budget should be as simple and require as little of your time as possible. If a system becomes bulky and time-consuming, it will usually be discarded. You should not be a slave to your budget; rather, your budget should be designed to serve you.

Before beginning a budget, give some thought to the options. The great French surgeon Nelaton once

> **You should not be a slave to your budget; rather, your budget should be designed to serve you.**

said, "If I had four minutes in which to perform an operation on which a life depended, I would take one minute to consider how best to do it."[9] It is tempting to quickly become convinced a budget is needed but fail to make sure it fits your needs. It is also important that a husband and wife are united on the system. This calls for communication. Many times budgets fail because a husband or wife gets excited about a particular kind of budget and fails to get his or her spouse to buy into the program. It takes more than one excited partner to make a budget work.

Another way to ensure failure is to attempt using the budget to force a spouse to change. If a system is going to help you reach a financial goal, it should always be agreed upon by both of you and put into action together.

So how do you find a system that fits your needs?

Computer-Driven Budgets

I have been asked by more than one young man if a person needs to buy a computer to have a budget. Be assured, budgets existed long before computers, and some of the most effective methods are very simple. There are some good computer programs for budgeting, and if you already use your computer on a daily basis for other tasks, this may be a good choice. But if you have never budgeted before, I would encourage you to start with a system that is not computer-driven to ensure you learn the concept. One of the primary purposes of a budget is to teach us how to make purchasing decisions. A budget tends to be neglected if it becomes too complicated, and if you are not comfortable with computers to start with, you will probably not be comfortable with a computer-driven budget either.

Allocation Method

All of us are familiar with a checkbook register. As money comes in, it is recorded in the deposit column, and as funds go out, they are recorded in the payment/debit column. On the right-hand side is a column for the balance. This balance is the amount currently available for use. The allocation method of budgeting works in a similar way. An allocation sheet, which looks much like a checkbook register, is created for each category in your budget: housing, transportation, etc. As money comes in each month, a certain amount is designated for each category and recorded on its respective allocation sheet. As you pay expenses throughout the month, the amount going out is deducted from the allocation sheet for that category. For example, if you write a $500 check for rent, you would also deduct $500 from the allocation sheet for housing.

Remember, one of the primary purposes of a budget is to control spending. With the allocation method of budgeting, a person can look at the allocation sheets at any time during the month and see how much money is still available in each category.

For example, suppose bicycles are on sale in town, and you have a child who has wanted one for some time. However, you are not sure you can afford one now. If you are using the allocation method, you can check your allocation sheet for recreation and see how much money is available. This provides guidance and assists you in making these types of decisions.

Envelope System

The envelope system has been around for many years and is still very effective. It works similarly to the allocation method except cash is used instead of a checkbook. The envelope system is simple to understand. After you have laid out your budget and have agreed how much money is to go into each category every pay period, you convert your paycheck into cash. Each category is given an envelope, and the appropriate amount of cash is then placed in each envelope. For example, if your weekly paycheck is $400 and you have decided to use 15 percent of your income for groceries, you would put $60 in an envelope for groceries.

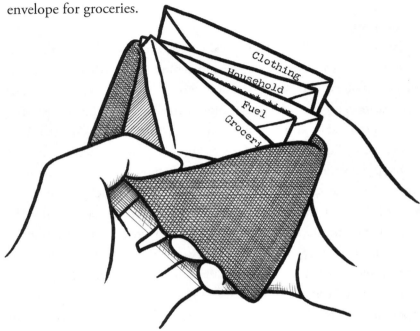

As the month goes by, money to pay for expenses is taken from the envelopes. If you are wondering, for example, how much money is available for clothing, you can look in the envelope designated for clothing and instantly know. This method, like the allocation method, allows you to move money from one category to another. If you have some out-of-state company one month and there isn't enough in the grocery envelope to purchase the needed food, some money can be taken from another envelope to cover the shortfall.

Build Your Budget to Fit

These are just a few of the options, and they can be altered to fit your circumstances. Many people, for example, choose to use the envelope system for items they normally spend cash for and the allocation method for things they prefer to pay by check. This keeps them from carrying large amounts of cash, yet allows them to use cash for items when it is simpler.

I feel it is best for most young couples to start by using cash for as much as possible. There is something about using actual money in transactions that helps teach the reality of how expensive operating a home really is. Somehow debit cards and checkbooks tend to insulate us from reality. As I mentioned in the chapter on consumer debt, studies consistently show we spend less when using cash.

Conclusion

There is no program or system that will fit every circumstance and situation. But it is important to find a method that fits your family's needs. If you are looking for a plan to start budgeting, contact the publisher and ask for *Budgeting Made Simple*. This is a simple budgeting system that our family has used for many years, and it may help you with that first step.

It is imperative that one of you be in charge of your budget and take responsibility for keeping it current. Both husband and wife need to be actively involved in setting up a budget and in discussing necessary changes. But it will work best if you can come to an agreement as to which one of you will be in charge of the record keeping. Budgeting need not be complicated or time-consuming. If you are spending more than an hour a month on your budget, you should probably review your method, for if it becomes cumbersome, you will probably stop using it.

Study Questions

1. Why is it important to keep a budget simple?

2. Discuss some scenarios in which a budget could drive a wedge in a marriage and actually make a relationship worse. What could cause this?

3. What could be some practical advantages or disadvantages to using the allocation method?

4. What could be some practical advantages or disadvantages to using the envelope system? If you have had experience with this, share your experiences.

5. Why is it important for one individual to be in charge of a family budget?

Chapter Twenty
Budgeting Challenges

F rank called late in the afternoon, his voice filled with appre-
hension. Something was obviously wrong. I had spent consid-
erable time with Frank on the phone before, and I could tell
he was greatly concerned. Frank didn't live in our local congregation,
yet I knew from past discussions that he had an ongoing battle with
consumer debt. He and his wife knew they were in trouble and had
put a basic budget together. They had worked hard at overcoming
their consumer debt issue, but progress was slow. They both knew
they needed to reduce their spending even more, and every time they
sat down to discuss ways to focus more of their money on the consumer debt, they ran into the same problem. The issue had become
the proverbial elephant in the room. They both knew it was there, but
they didn't talk about it.

Frank's wife had a hobby that was fairly expensive and was cost-
ing them a couple hundred dollars a month. This represented a good
amount of their discretionary money, yet it was very important to
Frank's wife. Every time Frank looked at the budget, his eyes went
to that hobby. If only she would give this up, their debt could be
overcome that much faster. But Frank was certain that bringing it up
would get him nowhere. This was something his wife had longed to
be involved in from childhood. She was finally fulfilling her dream.

Days and months had gone by and still they hadn't talked about it.
But though there was no discussion, the topic never left Frank's mind.
Like persistent dripping water, the issue continued to annoy and an-
ger him. Finally Frank decided he had been patient long enough. That

morning, during a disagreement about a trivial issue, he had taken the lid off his frustration and let his wife have it. Frank had released the building steam and informed his wife that she was being selfish and that this debt was simply a result of her unwillingness to give up her hobby. Then he had stomped out the door.

It was late in the afternoon now, and Frank was apprehensive about returning home. A more subdued and humble Frank was now on the phone asking for advice and prayer. He knew his wife's hobby wasn't really the only reason for their debt. He knew he had overstated his case, and he was also painfully aware that he had been stubborn in refusing to give up some things in his own life to help out. Frank knew the real problem was a failure to communicate properly with his wife. So after some discussion and prayer, a humble Frank headed home. His loving, repentant attitude helped restore the relationship so they could talk openly about their financial struggles. As he admitted his own weaknesses and showed a willingness to give up his hobbies, he found his wife more willing to give up hers.

Working Together in Love

If our homes are going to be successful in pursuing a Kingdom-building vision, it will take continual working together in love. We often say that opposites attract. We see this many times in marriage. Someone outgoing who loves to be the life of the party tends to marry someone more subdued and reserved. It is as though we admire qualities in a potential mate that we secretly long for in our own lives. But it is amazing how often this phenomenon occurs in marriages with regard to finances. One spouse tends to enjoy planning ahead, and the other lives to enjoy the day. One feels it is important to keep accurate records, and the other sees no need to be so fussy about details.

It is extremely important to our finances, and even more so to our marriages, that we not begin to view each other as adversaries. If your marriage is going to shine to the world for Jesus Christ, you will need to be companions, not combatants. Money is rarely

> **Money is rarely neutral in a marriage. It will either bind you together or drive you apart.**

neutral in a marriage. It will either bind you together or drive you apart. If you are going to be drawn together, you must have good, open communication. Talk about your differences. Be open regarding your feelings. Satan would love to bind this part of your life and make it ineffective for the Kingdom.

Get a vision of what a home can become when there is open communication. Imagine the possibilities in a home where a family is united in their focus on building the Kingdom and where every financial decision is viewed in the light of honoring Jesus Christ. Keep this vision before you. It takes tremendous self-denial to follow a Kingdom vision in the midst of a society going the opposite direction. But take courage. Many homes today are rising to the challenge, and your home can be one of them if you are willing to work together in love.

The Unexpected

"We were just starting to get things together, and then the transmission went out!" I have heard many statements similar to this. It may not have been the transmission, but something unexpected came up and the budget fell apart. Often these expenses are beyond our control. Medical bills, car repairs, appliance failures, or even loss of income—these are unexpected events all of us face. How can we prepare for these unexpected circumstances?

- **Pray and trust.** There is no way we can prepare for every possibility, and trying to do so will keep us from sharing and building the Kingdom. Fear of the unknown can immobilize us and make us ineffective. This does not mean we should never plan or use the minds God gave us. But trying to prepare for every unknown contingency will greatly hinder our effectiveness in the Kingdom.

- **Save for known expenses.** We know some of our larger expenses are coming. If we know, for example, that property taxes or insurance premiums need to be paid at a certain time during the year, then steps should be taken to save. Many couples forget about these larger expenses and then are shocked when the bills appear.

There is peace in knowing a little money each month is being set aside for these larger expenses.

- **Save for the inevitable.** If you drive a vehicle, you know you will face repairs and replacement eventually. If you wait until these expenses are due, you will probably face bills much larger than you are capable of paying that month. Many people are making car payments or paying off credit cards today simply because they failed to plan ahead. Later we will discuss some ways this can be done. When driving in heavy traffic, we were taught to look as far ahead as possible to watch for brake lights. If you are only watching the car in front of you, you may not have time to stop. The same is true in our financial lives. It pays to give some thought to what is coming down the road and plan accordingly.

- **Encourage brotherhood.** Unexpected expenses, such as medical emergencies, should be shared by our communities. We need to be actively involved in assisting each other during these times. Few things build brotherhood like sharing burdens. It can also be a wonderful witness to unbelievers. A brother in our congregation was traveling out of state and experienced car trouble. It was serious enough that he had to find another vehicle to travel on to his destination. Later, when he returned to pick up his repaired vehicle, the manager of the repair shop had a message for him. "Your bill has already been paid. In fact, several people have called, and they wanted to pay the entire bill for you anonymously." The manager concluded by saying, "I sure wish I had friends like you have." What an opportunity for this brother to humbly explain why he had friends like this! What an open door to share the blessing of Jesus and how He can change lives! Right in the middle of a self-centered society which views the dollar as king, we can demonstrate something different. We need to encourage sharing among ourselves and look for opportunities to help others with unexpected expenses.

Before leaving the topic of unexpected expenses, I think it is important to reiterate the importance of prayer and trust. Even though I believe it is right to encourage saving for some of these expenses, we need a strong realization that we can never save enough to cover every unknown. Older believers sometimes fall into the trap of worrying about their declining years. Will they have enough? Stop for a moment and consider.

How much do you think you would need to have in the bank to protect you from all the things that might happen? Imagine how ineffective the church would be if every believer attempted this. This is why our Lord Jesus spent so much time teaching us to trust our Father. He knows our needs and is fully capable of providing.

Impulse Buying

Another challenge to any budget is impulse purchases. Many of us have a weakness for buying items we were not originally planning to purchase. We come home from town with various "good" deals, saying things like:

"It was on sale."

"This is something I have always wanted."

"I don't really need it, but it would make a great gift."

"I was going to buy it sometime anyway."

"I just felt like buying it at the time."

All these statements may be true, but they are ignoring a basic truth. You didn't need it. Before we leave for the store, most of us make a list of the items we really need. But some of us have difficulty staying with the list. This can be devastating to a budget. If you struggle with impulse buying, consider the following ideas.

- **Sit down with your list and your spouse before leaving to shop.** Confess your weakness and ask for accountability. Doing this a few times may help you learn to make a complete list before leaving and never deviate from it.

- **Fill out an impulse-buying list.** You and your spouse agree to write down any item either of you would like to purchase; then you review the list thirty days later. Suppose a husband is looking at a sporting goods advertisement and suddenly becomes interested in buying a canoe. The price is good, it would be a good activity for the family, and the children are excited about it. You would take a piece of paper and write down the date, a description of the item, and the price. Thirty days later you would sit down again and talk about canoes. If you agree that it would bless your family and coincide with your vision of Kingdom building, then go ahead and buy the canoe. However, if you are like most impulse buyers, you will already have added some other items to the list after you became enthused about canoeing, and the canoe will have lost its original luster. Writing items down and waiting helps focus your resources on items and pursuits that are important and actually part of your overriding vision.

- **Avoid unnecessary shopping trips.** We will address this topic again, but it is so important when attempting to overcome the impulse-buying habit. If you struggle with impulse buying, understand that marketers are looking for people like you. Signs, music, and sales techniques are all designed to influence your decision making. The most effective way to win this battle is to avoid temptation as often as possible.

- **Avoid the price factor.** Just because an item is cheap does not mean it is good, needed, or useful. Many of us drag things home simply because they were cheap. An unneeded item is expensive, regardless of what you paid for it.

> **An unneeded item is expensive, regardless of what you paid for it.**

Budgeting With a Variable Income

Many people have difficulty budgeting due to the fact that their incomes vary from month to month. Perhaps you are paid by commission, and some months' sales are good and others are bad. Or maybe you do landscaping and have almost no income for several months each winter. Regardless of the cause, variable income can create havoc in a budget. How can you plan if you don't know how much is coming in? Each situation is different, but I want to give you two ideas that may help.

- Always separate your business income and business-related expenses from your household funds, even if it is just a small sideline business. This will require two separate checking accounts, but it is essential that you keep business and personal money separate. This is important for budgeting, and you will also find it beneficial at tax time.

- Find the average net income from your business and write a check each month from your business account to your personal account. It is important to make this amount as low as possible so your business can continue functioning if it does not produce as much income as anticipated.

If you are just starting a small home business, it is also important to remember to set aside some money for income tax. If you are not paying estimated income tax through the year, that tax can come as a rude awakening.

Conclusion

Your budget will experience challenges, but if you have a clear Kingdom vision for your family's finances, you will find blessing along the way. Many people whose financial situation looked impossible are able to share today how the Lord has delivered them. They committed their finances to the Lord, got serious about monitoring expenses, and now they are living productive, debt-free lives.

But make no mistake; successfully using a budget to manage your finances and climb out of debt is not easy. It will take commitment, communication, and strong resolve. But the blessing of finally seeing less money consumed selfishly and more flowing toward building the Kingdom is well worth the sacrifice.

Study Questions

1. Discuss the importance of husbands and wives being companions rather than combatants. How can we keep this goal alive in our marriages? Share some instances when you have failed in this.

2. How can we find the balance between saving for every future fear on the one hand, and forgetting to plan at all on the other? Share times when you have failed on either end.

3. Why is it so important for business and personal finances to be separate?

4. Share some instances in which you have fallen into the trap of buying on impulse. How did this affect your marriage?

5. How can a clear overriding vision of using resources for the Kingdom help overcome and avoid budgeting struggles?

CHAPTER TWENTY-ONE
The Two-Income Temptation

Recently in the United States, as well as in other industrialized countries, there has been an awakening. Parents who have been breathlessly racing to work each morning and wearily returning in the evening to children who have been alone all afternoon are wondering if it's worth it. They have been taught by society that a nice home, an upscale neighborhood, nice vehicles, and recreational toys for the weekend are worth the rat race. But parents are discovering they hardly know their children. A study conducted in Britain found the average working couple was only spending about nineteen minutes a day looking after their children.[10] Many children come home each day to an empty house, and the television has become their primary mentor. They are bounced around between school, daycare, and baby-sitters, and the resulting turmoil is destroying the family structure.

If you ask the parents in most of these homes, they do not feel good about it. Organizations like WMAG (Working Moms Against Guilt) have sprung up trying to soothe the remorse mothers feel. They know that leaving their children is not the best, but they feel helpless. They are caught in the current of prevailing wisdom, and strong social pressures keep them running. With the high cost of real estate, the ever-rising costs of operating a home, and all the additional expenses required to live in an industrialized nation, we are being told that two incomes are required. You just can't do it on one income anymore, people say. Things are different now.

But is this really true? Is it possible today to raise a family on just one income? Is Grandpa right when he says, "It's not the high cost of living young families are struggling with, but the cost of high living"? Let's begin by looking at a few facts regarding a two-income home purely from a financial viewpoint.

- Daycare costs. Increasing daycare costs greatly decrease the net amount generated by a second income. Some mothers are almost trading dollars with daycare costs alone. In addition, there are transportation and associated expenses.

- Food costs. The vast majority of two-income families spend far more on food than do those with stay-at-home mothers. Eating out and prepared foods become more common and are ways to relieve rat-race stress.

- Home upkeep. Most working mothers at some point resort to hiring a housekeeper. When Saturday finally comes, a mother who has neglected her children all week feels that time with the children is of greater importance than cleaning.

- Taxes. While additional income is taxable, reduced spending is not. Because of this, potential additional income from a second paycheck can be an illusion. Some accountants have observed that many mothers could better help their families financially if they spent their time and energy gardening, canning, and preparing home-cooked meals.

This list could go on. Additional clothing expenses may be an issue for women whose jobs are in the public eye. Many have concluded that, financially, they are not gaining much by having the mother work away from home. But so far we have dealt only with the financial question. If finances are all we are considering, often a family can increase their net income by having both parents work. But hopefully we are viewing life issues such as this one from more than just a financial viewpoint. One of my concerns when I see young mothers leave the home in an effort to increase income is the shift of focus and vision. Is it possible that we sacrifice our children in our quest for a higher level of living?

Fifty-Year Picture

Life is extremely short, and there is so much our children need to be taught and so little time in which to do it. Fifty years from now, whether you lived in a large home or a small one will be of little importance. Whether you owned your home or rented will not be so significant. In fifty years, will it really matter what model car you drove? But whether or not your child has gained a vision for living for the Lord Jesus will be of utmost importance and have eternal value. If you can show your children the value of the eternal and the emptiness of the temporal, it will be worth every sacrifice.

The Apostle Paul in his letter to Titus said the aged women in the church should teach the younger women "to be sober, to love their husbands, to love their children, to be discreet, chaste, keepers at home, good, obedient to their own husbands, that the word of God be not blasphemed."[a]

In this passage Paul instructs the young women to be "keepers at home." What was Paul saying? For many years there was no question. Believers universally understood that Paul was teaching that a woman was to stay at home—that working outside the home would betray her first calling, that of teaching and training her children.

However, as pressure from our materialistic culture has had its influence, the wording has been called into question. Some have said "keepers at home" does not mean she needs to stay at home, but rather that she should simply be a keeper, or a guard, of the home. That if she decides to work away from home, she should not neglect her duties as a mother and wife. But this reinterpretation is weak at best. In a time when Satan is using every method he can to infiltrate our homes, the best guard of a home is a mother in the home. Giving up time at home with the children simply to gain more of what our culture offers is a shortsighted tradeoff.

> **. . . the best guard of a home is a mother in the home.**

---

[a]Titus 2:4-5

The Provider

Throughout the Bible God has given man the responsibility to be the primary breadwinner for the family. It was Adam, not Eve, who was told by God he would earn his bread by the sweat of his brow. Since that time it has been primarily the husband's responsibility to provide for the family. In fact, Paul, when writing to Timothy, went so far as to say that "if any provide not for his own, and specially for those of his own house, he hath denied the faith, and is worse than an infidel."[b] While this verse is primarily speaking of assisting the elderly, Paul obviously put a high value on taking this responsibility seriously. God intends that we fathers provide for our homes and demonstrate to our children that income is produced by labor. He wants us to be diligent and willing to faithfully labor each day.

Men have an important role to fill in the home and in the workforce that encompasses more than just bringing home a paycheck. As a father goes out each morning, he comes in contact with many others and has the opportunity of sharing and caring throughout the day. When he returns home, he comes back with real-life stories and examples to share with his family regarding the blessing of following the Lord and the folly of chasing the world. A wise father is doing more each day than providing money. He is also providing a daily Christ-centered worldview to his family. The jobsite is a place where he can share the Gospel and encourage the saints. The father is called to be the natural and spiritual provider for the home.

The Protector

I like to think of the mother as the protector of the home. She is called to protect what her husband provides. Proverbs 31 says it like this, "The heart of her husband doth safely trust in her." The husband knows she is on guard at home and protecting what he is providing. Consider this in two areas.

- Financially. A wife is called to protect what her husband brings home. This means she is doing everything she can to exercise frugality in the home. She actively stretches

[b]1 Timothy 5:8

that paycheck as far as she can. She cheerfully receives the money he provides and goes about her job of using it carefully so the family's overriding vision can be reached.

- Spiritually. A godly wife has the responsibility to protect and defend the home. She is on the front line in the daily battle against the foe. She will be the one screening the unwholesome material and advertisements that flood the mailbox. During the day she will have opportunities to reinforce and support the teaching that Father provided the evening before. She is called to protect and guard the home with constant prayer.

When a home has a godly husband and a faithful wife each filling their respective places as provider and protector, there is tremendous potential. As they pursue their vision of building in the Kingdom of Jesus Christ, their home becomes a mission station in a foreign land and a great encouragement to others who have become sick of society's fixation on materialism.

When a family chooses to live on a single income and trust God to see them through the difficulties, I believe they are choosing God's best. They may not be able to travel like others, and there will be various pleasures which will always be beyond their grasp, but this kind of home will also be attended by blessings money can't buy.

Conclusion

Before we leave this topic, it is only fair to address times and circumstances in which it is necessary for a mother to work outside the home. Situations sometimes require a mother to go out and earn income simply for survival. I believe the local church should do everything possible to assist in these situations. Financial assistance is a small price to pay if it allows a mother to stay in her home with her children. May the Lord give us wisdom in these special circumstances.

But in most situations, women are not in the workplace for survival. Rather, there is a longing for more things and a desire to keep up with the surrounding culture. This is understandable when people are admittedly chasing present pleasure, but extremely sad when we as professing Christians fall for this logic. May the Lord bless your home as you put your energy and focus into building the Kingdom and spreading the Gospel where you have been called.

Study Questions

1. Why are some couples able to live on one income while others seem to need two? Are there times when two incomes are justified?

2. Are those of us who are older putting pressure on those who are younger by our lifestyles? Are we subtly teaching them that a higher level of living is normal? Are we "forcing" them to have two incomes to achieve this?

3. Are the older women in your congregation doing a good job of teaching the younger sisters? Are they doing this verbally as well as by example?

4. In what ways is the husband called to provide for his home? How is the wife called to protect?

5. How should the church respond to a single mother in a congregation? Should she be required to leave her home to produce an income?

CHAPTER TWENTY-TWO
The Marketing Minefield

We have all been there. After pushing a shopping cart around the grocery store, we finally arrive at the checkout only to find the lane closed. Blocking progress is a small child on the floor screaming as though his liver has just been removed without anesthetic. A harried mother rushes around trying to find something to pacify Johnny. The pathetic scene makes us somewhat ashamed of the human race.

We try to look away, a little embarrassed, as though in some way we are party to this fiasco. Sometimes Johnny is shouted into submission, but more often than not, he gets what he wants. And what was it he wanted? A little box of Super Sugar Bombs in a pretty package someone had placed right at his eye level. Who would do this? Who would put shelves of candy twenty-four inches off the floor where hundreds of little Johnnies stand beside their mothers every day?

The answer to this question should be a warning to every shopper. Great effort and vast amounts of money have been expended in an effort to cause you, the consumer, to purchase items you hadn't planned to buy. Many studies have been done to find out what will cause you to choose an item. Colors and types of packaging are analyzed closely, and great thought has been given to the moods created as shoppers consider products. If you are serious about staying within your budget, it is imperative you give some thought to the deception used in marketing; and make no mistake—we are surrounded by deceptive marketing.

Consumers in the Crosshairs

From the outer appearance of a store to the atmosphere within, every attempt is made to encourage relaxation. Consider the local grocery store. Grocery marketers know most individuals come to a grocery store intending to stay within their budgets. Marketing isn't easy. After all, most wives go grocery shopping every week, and after a housewife has spent more than she planned several weeks in a row, it becomes more difficult to make her do it again. This is the reason so much care is taken to provide a relaxed environment. The music is soft, the displays are attractive, a person greets you at the entrance, and many stores give out free samples. The goal is to disarm you and assure you that they are on your side. But be forewarned. When you enter a grocery store, you are entering a battlefield, and the individuals behind the scenes are not looking out for your interests.

> **When you enter a grocery store, you are entering a battlefield . . .**

To help prepare for the onslaught against your budget, let's look at a few techniques and marketing tactics you can expect in the battle.

- Loss leaders. A marketer's first challenge is to draw you into the store. A buyer won't spend unless he is in the store. Luring you in is the goal, and that is why our mailboxes and newspapers are filled with costly advertisements. Many times these flyers use loss leaders to draw you in. A loss leader is a product or service being sold at a lower price than the store pays. Most stores are willing to lose on a product to bring people into the store.

  Companies such as Gillette use this type of marketing. They are willing to essentially give their razor units away, knowing customers will have to buy the profit-making replacement blades. This strategy is frequently used in stores. A product is sold below the store's cost in an attempt to get you into the store, knowing that once they get you in, you will probably buy more.

- Store layout. Once you have been drawn into a store by a sale or a loss leader, you will almost always observe something else of interest. The product which brought you in is rarely close to the entrance. In fact, products such as milk, bread, meat, and cheese, which we all use regularly, will almost always be found in the back or sides of the store. An amazing amount of research has gone into store layout, and everything in a grocery store is placed there by design. One of the marketer's goals is to keep the consumer in the store as long as he can and to cause the buyer to walk past as many products as possible. If all you need is a loaf of bread and a gallon of milk, these tactics can be very frustrating. Marketers know that if they expose you to tempting products you hadn't previously considered, you will probably purchase more than you intended.

- Shelf space and product arrangement. We are more likely to buy products displayed at certain locations on the shelves. Products at eye level are more likely to be purchased than products that are up high or down low, and displays at the ends of aisles sell much more than items in the center. For this reason stores put higher-priced products and items which have a high percentage of profit in these high-profile areas. Costlier name-brand items are typically located at eye level while lower-priced generic products tend to be on lower levels. Nothing is left to chance, and the goal is to shake loose more of your money.

Becoming aware of marketing tactics can help you stay on track in budgeting. Stores are not seeking your advantage, and your financial well-being is not their primary concern. Stores are battlefields, and those who are wise will give some thought to enemy tactics. We cannot totally avoid stores. But it should be obvious that reducing time spent there will help you reach your financial goals. With this in mind, let's briefly consider recreational shopping.

Recreational Shopping

Americans love to shop, and the last few decades have seen a terrific escalation in malls, shopping centers, and factory outlets. In 1986 there were still more high schools than shopping centers in America, but less than fifteen years later there were more than twice as many shopping centers as high schools. Massive mega-malls have become destinations for family vacations. The number of people escaping to these huge shopping conglomerates for entertainment, pleasure, and relaxation exceeds the number of people visiting our national parks. There is no question; we live in a culture consumed by consumption. As one writer said, "The urge to splurge continues to surge."[11]

But is there really a place in a Christian's life for recreational shopping? Can a believer who is serious about financial stewardship really afford to shop just for entertainment? One of the sins listed by Paul in his letter to the Ephesians is covetousness. It is listed

> **Can a believer who is serious about financial stewardship really afford to shop just for entertainment?**

right there with idolatry and gross immorality. Do we have the same godly fear of covetousness that we have of sexual perversion or idol worship? What is covetousness?

The Princeton University Dictionary says covetousness is "an envious desire to possess something." It is a continual desire to possess things I don't have. Sometimes I fear that, having grown up in a capitalistic culture, I have become so used to this feeling that it fails to alarm me. This subtle inner longing for bigger, better, faster, nicer, and newer becomes so normal it doesn't seem wrong. All of us need to bring this area of our hearts before the Lord. We need to acknowledge that we live in a society that fosters discontent and accumulation. It is imperative that we take steps to guard against this disease in our own lives. This fight against covetousness will require constant diligence and refocusing on things of lasting value. This will not be easy.

Home-Decorating and Kitchen Parties

Another marketing scheme that encourages spending on unnecessary items is home-decorating and kitchen parties. These parties use friendships and the home setting as marketing tools. This is a marketer's dream. Sitting in the midst of peers and listening to friends discuss the virtues of the latest candle, basket, or kitchen item provides a strong peer pressure many women cannot withstand. Many high-quality products can be purchased at these parties, and there may be times this is expedient. But you are subjecting yourself to an environment where consumption of unnecessary items is encouraged.

I think Christians should ask themselves this question: Will recreational shopping or home-decorating and kitchen parties help me in this battle? Is it wise for the serious follower of Jesus, who is attempting to find fulfillment and contentment in Him alone, to purposely enter an environment designed to create discontent and increase consumption? I think the answer is obvious. We cannot afford to intentionally put ourselves in the path of temptation.

One final word of encouragement before leaving this topic. David the psalmist made this observation regarding choosing where we find our fulfillment. "Delight thyself also in the Lord; and he shall give thee the desires of thine heart."[a]

Many Kingdom Christians who have purposed to find their fulfillment in nothing other than the Lord Jesus can testify to the truth of this verse. Gradually the Holy Spirit has changed them, and as a result, their wants have changed. That inner desire for more earthly possessions has been transformed, and their greatest desire and delight is in the King and His Kingdom. In the past they found their wants gradually becoming needs. Now, as the Spirit works in their lives, they find that they do not want what they do not really need.

Winning the Battle

Most of us cannot avoid shopping. We need items from the store, so how can we avoid the marketing pitfalls and snares we confront while there? Here are some steps we can take to reduce temptation and avoid unnecessary spending.

[a]Psalm 37:4

- **Make a complete list.** It is very important to shop with a detailed list. When you leave home, your list should be so complete that you can be confident these items are all you need.

- **Follow your list exclusively.** Once you have a detailed and complete list to work from, stay with it. Ignore the smells in the deli section and the item you just sampled that tasted so good. You came to this store for a specific purpose, and your goal is to return home with only the items you came for. Occasionally, due to a special sale, it makes sense to alter the original plan. But these changes to your list should be made with care.

- **Limit your trips to town.** Some families have started making one major shopping trip per month. Some items, such as milk and bread, must be purchased more frequently, but reducing shopping trips has proved an effective way of reducing spending.

These three points are not intended to be exhaustive. On the contrary, entire books have been written on this topic. But if you really want to stick with a budget and reach a financial goal your family has set, it is important that you give thought to how you shop. Marketers love the casual shopper, and the longer they can keep you in their store, the more time they have to distract you. Retailers watch this. Some can even tell you how much money the average shopper will spend per minute spent in their store.

> **Marketers love the casual shopper . . .**

Conclusion

Remember, the shopping environment is not a neutral environment. Shopping centers and malls are intentionally planned, from the foundation to the signage, to foster excessive consumption. The modern store is a battlefield, and the unsuspecting shopper is the primary target. This should not alarm us, but it should cause us to reduce our exposure to temptation whenever possible. This can be accomplished by limiting trips to town and avoiding shopping for pleasure. But the most effective precaution of all is a transformed desire and a proper focus on possessions. Regardless of how they are marketed, the value-less trinkets in the marketplace will have little pull on the believer who is being led by the Spirit and is focused on building the Kingdom.

Study Questions

1. Share some experiences of when you were persuaded to purchase items you had not intended to buy. What did you learn from this? How has it affected your shopping habits?

2. In view of this chapter, why is it so important to limit trips to town? Share ways you have found to help decrease your exposure to marketing.

3. How can Psalm 37:4 provide a vaccine against wasteful spending? Can you share a victory the Lord has given you in this area? Perhaps something which once was very enticing but has now lost its appeal?

4. Share how lists have helped you stay within a budget.

5. When can home-marketing parties be a good way to purchase items? When can they encourage spending on the unnecessary and unneeded?

CHAPTER TWENTY-THREE
The Vehicle Dilemma

There was no question that this was a good deal. Sometimes a person can't be too sure, but this time it was obvious. As Timothy circled the minivan and listened to the salesman's pitch, he became more and more certain this was the van for him. He hadn't really planned on buying that day; he had just seen this van sitting on the lot while driving by and thought he would take a look. After admiring the minivan for a while, Timothy glanced back at the older vehicle he owned. The car had aged remarkably in the few minutes he had been here.

Timothy had paid his vehicle off several years ago and had intended to save money to purchase another. But somehow he hadn't been able to put much money together in the last two years. With a family of six boys, there just wasn't much extra money lying around. In fact, he probably didn't even have enough cash for a down payment on this van.

The salesman continued to sing the virtues of the van. Reluctantly, Timothy finally broke in on the salesman's song and confessed he had little money available. But Timothy need not have feared. As he told me later, the salesman was extremely helpful. Before Timothy knew what had happened, he was the owner of a new minivan. Well, not the sole owner. It would be five years and sixty payments before Timothy possessed a clear title.

A few days later I received a call from Timothy. The initial new vehicle euphoria was past, and it was a more subdued Timothy who told me the minivan story. The bottom line was that Timothy was discouraged. He was painfully aware that he had fallen into the trap again. Once more he had become ensnared in the endless cycle of debt, payments, and depreciation. He was suddenly remembering how tired he had become of car payments on the last vehicle, and now here he was again.

The Cycle

The car loan cycle works like this. You purchase a car on credit, make payments for five years, and then about the time the car is paid for, you decide it is time to purchase another, and the cycle continues. The loan remains long after the newness of the vehicle has worn off, yet the exciting memory of driving a new car remains. So you stop in to look. The salesman points out the fact that your car is getting older and it is not cheap to replace an engine or transmission. In fact, just last week someone was in the dealership's service department with a vehicle almost identical to yours needing major repairs. Somehow the car we are currently driving is always the model with suicidal tendencies.

This fear of major repairs, coupled with the vision of driving out with a new set of wheels, finally pushes us over the edge. "After all," I have heard people say, "if we are going to be paying a lot of money on repairs anyway, we may as well just make payments." But is this endless cycle necessary? Do we need to be in lifelong bondage to interest and payments? Is there a way to escape this endless cycle of borrowing?

The Way of Escape

Yes, there is a way out, if you are willing to take some steps and do some proactive planning. We are at different places in life, and our needs are different. But let's look at two common scenarios which young families face today and consider some proactive steps that can be taken to break this cycle of debt and repayment. Neither of these scenarios may exactly fit your situation, but hopefully by looking at these examples you can get a helpful picture.

The Reliable-Car Scenario

Let's start by looking at the family who has a good, reliable vehicle. We will assume this vehicle is paid for, has 80,000 miles on it, and needs no major repairs that we know of. Is it better to trade it in on a new one now while it has some value, or is it better to keep driving it? And if you keep driving it, how long do you do this? Until it needs costly repairs and the expense to fix it is more than the vehicle is worth? These are questions all of us deal with, and of course, we are dealing with many unknowns. It would be helpful to know ahead of time that this car was going to disintegrate at 85,000 miles. But you don't know. So what do you do?

First go back to your overriding vision for your home and finances. Reestablish in your mind your reason for having a vehicle. It is important to begin this decision-making process with pure motives and a proper perspective. If your present vehicle is providing the transportation you need, is there another reason you desire one that is nicer and newer? Be sure you are being honest before proceeding.

After you have reestablished vision and purpose for your vehicle, you need to acknowledge that it is a perishable item and will have to be replaced sometime. It is losing value. It will only start so many times, and each time you fire it up there is one less start left in it.

Most of us look at the gas gauge before leaving on a trip. We want to know whether or not there is enough gas to take us to our destination, and if there isn't, we make sure we have enough money with us to refill along the way.

In the same way, we need to make some preparation for vehicle replacement. In our scenario the vehicle has 80,000 miles, and assuming this vehicle is average, there are still quite a few miles left. If you trade it in now, you will be making payments (which is what you are trying to avoid) and dealing with a higher rate of depreciation, which we will talk about later. So let's just say you decide to keep your vehicle and start planning for replacement.

I recommend that people who are planning for replacement set a mileage target at which they plan to exchange vehicles. Let's suppose you decide to drive this vehicle until it has 150,000 miles on it. You will need to estimate the amount your vehicle will be worth when it has 150,000 miles on it, and how much it will cost to purchase another vehicle. Let's assume you estimate your old vehicle will have a value of $4,000 and the two-year-old used vehicle you are planning to replace it with will cost $16,000. This means you will need to have $12,000 when it is time to replace your vehicle.

In this scenario, if you are going to escape the vehicle payment cycle, you are going to need to save $12,000. Maybe this looks impossible to you, but here is how I suggest you save this money. In the situation above, you have 70,000 miles left on your old vehicle until you need the $12,000. If you divide $12,000 by the 70,000 miles you plan to drive, you will come up with 17 cents per mile. This is the amount per mile you need to set aside for replacement. This may seem like a lot to save each month, but it is probably less than a monthly payment on a new vehicle.

When we were first married, my wife and I determined to stay out of the monthly payment rat race. So on the first of each month, my wife would check the mileage on our vehicle to see how many miles we had driven during the last month. She would then multiply the number of miles by the amount we had agreed to save per mile and put that much in a savings account designated for car replacement. In the scenario we created above, if we drove 800 miles the previous month, we would multiply 800 by 17 cents and put $136 in a savings account for vehicle replacement. This money could also be used for repairs along the way. If we had more repairs than expected, we needed to drive the old car a little longer.

As my wife and I used mileage in our early years of marriage to determine savings, we began to think of driving differently. Suddenly it became painfully obvious that driving was directly affecting our budget. If we lived twelve miles from town and were setting aside 17 cents per mile, a trip to the grocery store cost us $4.08 before adding the cost of fuel. We began planning our trips to avoid unnecessary runs.

You may be thinking there is no way you can find another $136 in your budget right now. Remember, these numbers can be altered. You can change the amount per mile by either driving the vehicle you have a little longer or lowering the purchase price of the vehicle you plan to buy. But you will find peace of mind in having some money set aside for repairs and replacement.

The Old-Car Scenario

The second situation we want to look at is what I call the old-car scenario. Maybe your old car already has 150,000 or even 200,000 miles on it and you have no money saved for replacement. First of all, you are to be congratulated on avoiding the new-car monthly payment cycle. Second, if you are going to continue avoiding the payment cycle, you need to start saving quickly. Maybe you don't think this is possible, but I like to tell people who are in this dilemma to just pretend for a while their old car is a new one. Go ahead and start making payments to a savings account and imagine that Bank of America is going to call if even one payment is missed. Don't be afraid to get some accountability from a brother in your congregation who shares your vision.

You will have some repairs along the way, but in almost every case you are better off keeping your old vehicle as long as possible. Sometimes during this process of saving for a replacement vehicle, you may find yourself facing a repair bill that does not seem feasible considering the value of your old vehicle. In this situation it may be best to use the money you have saved to purchase an older vehicle that will work while you continue to save. But if at all possible, avoid getting into the monthly payment trap. Like most snares in life, it is easy to get into, but hard to get out of.

You will notice in both of these scenarios that I recommend keeping the old vehicle as long as possible. This is almost always the best from a financial point of view, and many times our problem is simply the fact that we want more than transportation. Our needs are different, and some of us drive long distances on a regular basis and need dependability. But dependability can become an excuse for borrowing or buying more car than we need. It is important, once again, that we go back to our overriding vision. Talk about it frequently. Are we still serious about putting God's Kingdom first, and do we still desire, as a family, to make each decision in light of our overriding vision? It is very easy to say we have a Kingdom vision for our family, but it is harder to live out this vision when it means driving a vehicle that is disdained by society and sometimes even our friends.

Vehicle Depreciation

As we all know, a vehicle depreciates very rapidly the first year and then loses its value more slowly as time goes on. The University of Michigan did a study on vehicle depreciation which revealed that the average vehicle on the market loses about 37 percent of its value in the first year and 27 percent of the remaining value the second.[12] If you look at the chart below, it will give you an idea how much value

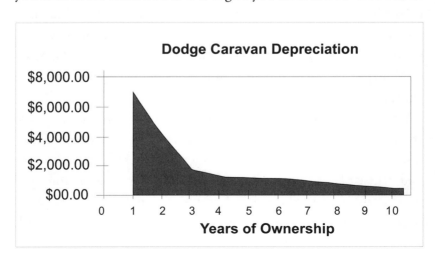

a vehicle loses each year. This chart is based on a Dodge minivan, and while each vehicle will be a little different, this shows how the rate of depreciation changes as a vehicle ages.

You can see the vehicle is losing about $7,000 the first year it is on the road, and around $4,000 the second year. This means you should be able to find a two-year-old Dodge Caravan for around $11,000 less than its original selling price.

Jewelry on Wheels

Vehicles today are much more reliable than they were thirty years ago, and this is a great blessing for those who are purchasing a vehicle just for transportation. Yet though they last longer than they used to, they still depreciate at a rapid rate. Why is this? Why are people willing to lose so much in the first several years of ownership? Why are they willing to pay so much just to drive a new vehicle?

While there may be some exceptions, the fact is many are buying more than transportation when purchasing a vehicle. Vehicles are used to project an image. Many of us who would never think of adorning ourselves with jewelry can be tempted to draw attention to ourselves with the vehicles we drive. This is an area we each need to bring before the Lord. Is my choice of vehicles consistent with my verbal assent to a Kingdom vision? Am I wasting goods that could be used in God's Kingdom because of an inner desire to project a certain image?

> **Many of us who would never think of adorning ourselves with jewelry can be tempted to draw attention to ourselves with the vehicles we drive.**

While we each need to examine our own lives in this area, we also need to be cautious about judging our brother's needs. We are all in different situations, have different spouses, and have differing needs. Some congregations have agreed not to purchase new vehicles in an attempt to focus more on the Kingdom, while others have left this decision up to the individual. This seems to be an area of enough importance that, at the very least, we should be discussing it in our congregations. If we can encourage each other to make Kingdom choices, it could free up money to bless others.

Conclusion

It seems obvious that if we are going to use vehicles that depreciate rapidly and need occasional repairs, we need to put forth some effort in planning. Some thought needs to be given to replacement. We also need to encourage each other in our vehicle choices. If someone in your congregation is making an obvious choice to drive an older car, encourage him. This is another area where those who are older and perhaps no longer facing financial strain can have a wonderful influence on young families. Making a conscious decision to continue driving the same older vehicle for a few more years can greatly bless those who are younger. If you are in this older age group, you have an opportunity to voluntarily reduce your consumption and show the younger families in your congregation that you really believe what you profess.

Study Questions

1. What can we learn from Timothy's method of shopping for a van? What mistakes did he make?

2. Do people in your congregation feel pressure to purchase a certain type or model vehicle? Would they be comfortable driving an older vehicle to worship services?

3. When would buying a new vehicle be appropriate for a business?

4. Why are we willing to lose so much those first few years to drive a new vehicle? Can a vehicle be more than just transportation to you?

5. Discuss the differing needs in each home and the need to have charity among ourselves as we observe each other's decisions. How does Romans 14:4 relate to this?

CHAPTER TWENTY-FOUR
Planning for Future Expenses

I clearly remember the phone call from the accountant. It was just a routine call for him, letting one of his many clients know how much he owed the IRS in taxes next month on April 15. But the amount hit me like a bombshell! I wasn't prepared at all. Suddenly my cozy little financial life turned upside down and took my stomach with it. I was sure there must be a mistake, but there wasn't.

I had no excuses, at least not any good ones. This tax was based on my revenue, and I couldn't argue with the fact I had received the income. The numbers were there to prove it. I had fallen into the same trap many self-employed people fall into after their first year of business.

We made the transition from being employed by others to being self-employed early in our marriage. Suddenly income tax wasn't automatically removed from my check. I had been told to plan for income tax but hadn't given it a lot of thought. I was focusing on survival, hoping the business was successful enough to stay afloat. The thought of making enough to owe significant taxes wasn't a primary concern.

As extra money came in, we just tucked it in savings and began to think of things this money could buy. We didn't have much, and it wasn't difficult to think of items we would like to purchase. There wasn't a large pile in savings that first year, but it was enough to let us dream. But as our savings slowly increased, something else changed. Now we weren't as desperate. Money began to flow out a little more freely. Things we didn't think we could afford before looked more feasible.

Then this unexpected phone call came and abruptly, almost to the dollar, all the money we had saved during the last year was gone. Suddenly being in business wasn't so fun anymore. Why work all year just to give the government everything we had saved? But really, all my frustration and annoyance was simply a result of failing to plan. If I had set aside a certain percentage with each paycheck, this would never have happened.

Known Expenses

Many expenses hit us unexpectedly. Emergency room visits, transmission failures, and travel expenses due to a death in the family are examples of costs we cannot always anticipate. But we know other expenses are coming, like property taxes, birthday and Christmas gifts, certain insurances, and if you are self-employed, income tax. These bills come at certain times of the year and are somewhat predictable. There are also expenses, such as travel, in which a certain amount of money may be needed at a particular time of the year. If we have been planning for these expenses, it is much easier to stay on track with our budgeting. Too often we allow these types of expenses to surprise us throughout the year.

Playing Dodge "Bill"

Most of us remember playing dodge ball in school. Children stood in a circle with one person in the center. If you were part of the outer ring, the goal was to hit the person in the middle with the ball, and if you were in the center, the goal was to dodge each ball. Most of us remember what it was like to be in the center. You had to move quickly, and it was always nice to have a little time to prepare for the coming ball. You would back away from the person preparing to throw so you had plenty of time to dodge. But as soon as the ball was thrown, you had to turn quickly because it would soon be coming from a new direction.

If you were in the ring of children attempting to hit the person in the middle, the faster you could move the ball around, the less time the person in the middle had to prepare and the greater chance you would hit him. There was no rest in the middle, and it took constant vigilance and agility to survive.

Trying to manage a family budget without planning for known

expenses can feel a little like trying to live in the center of a dodge ball game. Perhaps we should call it a dodge "bill" game. You become breathless and can never relax. About the time you recover from one surprise expense, another one hits you from behind. These surprises fill life with uncertainty and make it difficult to remain calm. I have heard people say, "We were just starting to get back on our feet, and suddenly we got hit with our property tax. Now we're in trouble again!"

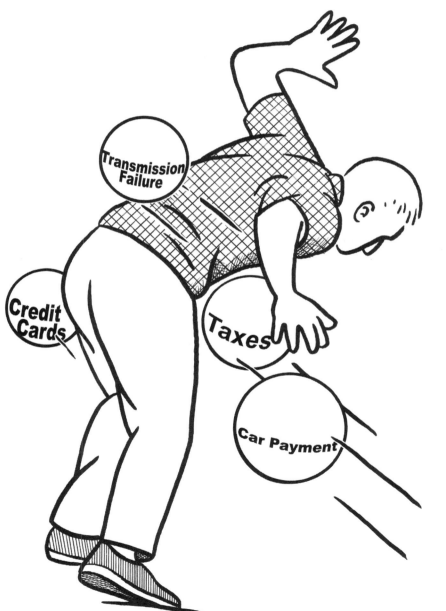

"So, you didn't know your property tax bill was coming?" I might ask, and most times they will reply, "Yes, we knew it was going to come, but in the middle of all the other expenses we were not expecting, we just forgot about it."

Planning for known expenses does not remove the bills, but it does make management of them much more enjoyable. Perhaps we could illustrate it this way. Most of us also remember playing kickball in school. We played this game with

> **Planning for known expenses does not remove the bills, but it does make management of them much more enjoyable.**

the same ball used in dodge ball, but there was a major difference between the games. While in dodge ball you never knew when or from what angle the ball might come, in kickball it was predictable. You waited at home plate while the ball rolled toward you down the same predictable path. You expected it and tried to be ready for it.

This is what planning for known expenses can do for you. Whether you are saving for car replacement or income tax, there is peace in being ready. You will never be prepared for every bill that comes at you, but if you can give some thought and preparation to those you know are coming, it can be a tremendous blessing to your home.

How Do We Plan for Known Expenses?

There are various methods to prepare for known expenses, but these methods have one thing in common. You will need to set a little money aside periodically in preparation for the expense. Like Joseph preparing for famine in Egypt, we know a time is coming when extra resources will be needed, so we begin planning for it now. For example, if you know you are going to need $1,000 one year from now for property tax, you might deposit $83 each month in a savings account in preparation. If you are self-employed and want to be ready when your income taxes are due, whether you are paying quarterly or yearly, you might want to deduct a percentage of each check that is transferred from your business to your personal checking and set this aside as well.

For plans like this to work, it must be understood that as you set this money aside, it is no longer yours. If you begin to withdraw money from these accounts simply because things are a little tight this month, you are likely to have trouble later. This type of planning takes discipline, but the resulting peace is worth it.

Preparing for the Unknown

We have looked at the blessing of setting money aside for known expenses, but what about the unknown? What about all those expenses we were totally unprepared for? Should we keep savings on hand just in case something happens?

Let your mind go for a moment. Imagine all the things that could happen in the next year. Think about the possibility of losing your job, a major economic meltdown, or an accident that could radically change your quality of life and destroy your ability to provide for your family. All these potential scenarios have happened to others and could happen to you. How can you prepare for all this?

Most of us have gone down this road before. Perhaps we have read an article predicting major economic upheaval or heard a discussion revealing inside information on an impending global catastrophe. It looks inevitable, and our way of life looks as if it might be destroyed abruptly. Suddenly we feel fingers of fear constricting our hearts. Peace goes out the door and panic comes in. Our minds are plagued with questions. If all this happens, what about food? And if all the utilities stop functioning, how would we even pump water? And what if . . .

What If . . .

Jesus had much to say regarding these fears and the "what if" scenarios that tend to plague us. He knows we live in an uncertain world and are tempted to fear. In the sixth chapter of Matthew, He directly addresses worrying about the unknown. "Your heavenly Father knoweth that ye have need of all these things," Jesus said regarding food and drink. "But seek ye first the kingdom of God, and his righteousness; and all these things shall be added unto you."[a]

---

[a]Matthew 6:32-33

What was Jesus saying in this chapter? He warned against laying up treasures and giving thought to tomorrow. What did He mean? Was He saying it is wrong to plan for the unknown? Is God disappointed when we save for future unknown expenses?

I first want to confess my inadequacy in answering these questions. Perhaps there isn't a packaged response which will answer each situation and fit every family's need. I have two burdens here. First, I want to be very careful about trying to reword the teachings of Jesus to fit my viewpoint. Second, it is important that we don't lay a greater burden on young families than Jesus intended.

We need to let these sayings of Jesus penetrate our hearts. If we feel uncomfortable when reading the Sermon on the Mount in the area of finance and find ourselves skimming over certain parts, we are probably trying to avoid God's message.

Our environment today is radically different from Jesus' time, and if we are going to make use of modern medicine, for example, some thought should be given to the potential cost. I believe it is wise, especially if we have debt, to have a little set aside for contingencies. I am reluctant to say how much we should save. I believe this amount should be decided on our knees and possibly with the help of a brother who knows our inclinations and personality. Some of us tend to save to the point of hoarding. Others struggle with lack of planning and are inclined to give inadequate attention to the future. They give too much thought to today and neglect to sow seed for tomorrow.

The bottom line of Jesus' teaching seems to be trust in our heavenly Father. Someone who is trying to stockpile enough treasure to insure him against any possible catastrophe does not trust his Father. But neither does someone who is spending money as fast as it comes in, knowing his congregation will bail him out if things get tough. Both are trusting something other than God.

Conclusion

Planning for future expenses is an area we need to discuss openly and honestly in our congregations. We also need to exhort and encourage one another. We will probably never get it all just right, and we need fervent charity among ourselves as we wrestle with it. Our tendency is to lean on things rather than on God Himself, and all of us are tempted to trust in less than the best. But where the future expense is known, I believe it is important to have a plan in place and be saving toward it. You will find that preparation brings peace, and lack of planning in this area brings constant chaos.

Study Questions

1. What are some known expenses we can prepare for? Share ways you have found to be prepared.

2. How does the account of Joseph in Egypt illustrate the need to give some thought to coming hardship? Was he storing grain due to a lack of faith?

3. What about saving for the unknown? Does God want us to keep a cash reserve for unknown expenses? If so, how much?

4. If we attempted to save for every potential coming expense, how much would we need to have in reserve? How does Matthew 6:25-34 apply to this?

5. Is trusting in our congregation to pay our bills different than trusting in a savings account? How is this different?

CHAPTER TWENTY-FIVE

Teaching Our Children About Money

G rowing up, I remember reading many stories of people who lived during the Great Depression. These were people who struggled with poverty right here in America. Food wasn't always plentiful and jobs were scarce. But as a young man, the part that always captured my attention was the role of children. Many of them played a vital part in helping the family survive.

One series of books many of us enjoyed reading was written by Ralph Moody. He told of his adventures as a youngster in Colorado when he and his siblings were trying to earn money to help their mother. It seemed they were always earning, growing, or saving something to be of assistance. Their father had died while the children were still young, and Ralph and his siblings knew if they were going to continue eating, a lot depended upon them. Sometimes they would sneak the money they had earned into the family cookie jar without telling their mother since she was concerned that they were working too hard. These children grew up with an eye on survival, daily doing everything they could to reduce costs and increase income. They were vital to the family and they knew it.

Looking back, I think one of the reasons we young men enjoyed these stories was because we also wanted to be significant. We longed to play an important role in our family's survival. As I read, I was putting myself in Ralph's place, working long hours, negotiating little deals with the neighbors, and finding ways to do without certain luxuries.

But I was only pretending; my life was much different. My father brought home enough income to buy all the food and clothes we needed. We even had a picture on the wall of orphans in some far-off country we were sending extra money to support. While my parents tried to keep me busy with jobs around the house, obviously I wasn't really needed for our family to survive. We had plenty.

Most of us have known nothing but plenty, and while some of us may have grown up on farms or in homes where our help was necessary, few of us felt needed for survival. We felt wanted, and at times helpful, yet we knew the family would probably make it without us.

Replicating Poverty

We still want our children to feel needed and significant, but we are not sure how to do this. We try home projects. We buy goats or a few cows, hoping the children will learn responsibility by doing chores. Or we grow some kind of produce for sale. We hope the constant weeding, pruning, and picking will keep them occupied and teach them a work ethic that will assist them later in life.

When my own children were young, we had an acre of red raspberries. This was no small undertaking. We have many good memories of working with them in the raspberry patch, and while some of those memories are better than others, everyone in our family today would agree it was a blessing. These types of activities are essential to helping our children understand that money comes from labor. Parents also quickly learn that working with their children instills motivation better than just telling them to do it.

But I think all of us also understand there is a big difference between raising a crop or cow *with* money and raising a crop or cow *for* money. Our children know when we are making work for them, and the bottom line is that it is difficult to imitate the

> **. . . there is a big difference between raising a crop or cow *with* money and raising a crop or cow *for* money.**

blessing of poverty. Our children do not feel the same about mucking out the cow pen when they sense the goal is a family project rather than survival. It is easier for all of us to labor toward a goal when we believe in the vision.

Personal Disclaimer

I understand the risk in trying to tell parents how to teach their children. In fact, if there are any two areas in which we tend to react negatively to advice, they are how to use our money and how to train our children. Yet I also believe our young families are asking for advice on both, so allow me to share a few suggestions. Take this from a parent who has failed miserably in some of these areas. It is much easier to write about how things should be done than to actually implement them in our homes. I encourage you to hold these suggestions up before the Lord in prayer, compare them to the Word, and let Him give you guidance.

Go back for a moment to your overriding vision for your home. What is it? If your vision is to use every resource your family possesses to build the Kingdom of Jesus Christ, I want to encourage you to instill this vision in your children at a young age.

Just as families during the Great Depression had a well-defined goal (survival), your home should also have a clear goal, and every choice should be made in light of this overriding vision. Therefore, prayerfully consider the following suggestions:

- **Communicate the vision often**. If your children understand your vision for your finances, they will be more enthusiastic about working together to reach a goal. Make them an integral part of building the Kingdom. Let them think of ways to save and places to spend. Discuss Satan's attempts to distract us from a godly financial vision. Be open about your own struggles in maintaining vision. If you have a weakness for a certain hobby and are tempted to spend money on this instead of the Kingdom, confess this and ask for prayer. Your children are also going to be tempted in this way. Show them how to properly deal with weaknesses and how to humbly ask for accountability.

- **Keep the target polished.** Again, use meal times and family devotions to discuss the needs your family wants to target. Maybe you have a widow living down the road, grandparents who need help around the house, or someone in your congregation who has a special need. Perhaps you just received a newsletter from an organization telling about street children in Nicaragua, a famine in Sudan, or persecuted Christians in China. Keep holding needs up before your family. This will help keep the vision clear and the target for your finances polished.

- **Discuss the connection between home projects and the target.** Children know when they are just being kept busy. But they will be much more interested and willing to help if they know why they are working. This is why many children voluntarily jumped out of bed early during the Great Depression. They recognized the connection between their own labor and the family's survival. In the same way, our children will enthusiastically go the second mile to make a home project work if they understand why they are doing it. For example, if the goats are being raised and sold to support school children in Haiti, they will be much more willing to take initiative in the project.

- **Be on the alert for hypocrisy.** Children have a great ability to sniff out hypocrisy. I believe the number one reason the suggestions listed above fail is due to a double standard in our homes. Our children will labor for a vision if the vision has value. But the child learns the worth of the vision by his parents' willingness to sacrifice for it. I cannot expect my children to become excited about a vision if it becomes obvious that I am unwilling to give up my hobby to reach it. It will be difficult to convince my children to keep getting up early so we can send Bibles to the persecuted church if they just saw me come home with a new speedboat.

Conclusion

Our children need to buy into our vision. For this to happen, the vision must have value. This occurred in many homes during difficult times in the past, but today it is different. Our grandparents didn't choose to work toward a vision; they were forced to. Today we have a choice. We can live for today and see how much pleasure we can wring out of this life, even in our conservative churches. Our standards are not too difficult. We can meet all these standards, be good Anabaptist church members, and still retain our own desires and self-centered visions.

But if we want our children to rise to a higher standard and learn to live for the Kingdom, it will take more than outward compliance to standards. These standards are important, but children need to see a higher level of self-denial in our lives. Our use of money tells children what we actually value the most, and we need the Lord's help to ex-emplify a godly financial vision and a lasting legacy.

Study Questions

1. What are some of the blessings children receive by growing up in poverty? Why is this hard to replicate in a home that is not poor?

2. Why is it important to share our weaknesses with our children and ask for their prayers?

3. How can keeping the needs of others before ourselves and our children help keep us focused on the goal of building the Kingdom? How will this affect thankfulness and contentment?

4. Share ideas on how we can connect our children to the vision of Kingdom building. What has worked in your home? Share ways in which you have failed in this.

5. Have your children ever reminded you when you have strayed from your verbal teaching in this area of stewardship?

Part Six
Staying on Track

CHAPTER TWENTY-SIX
Identifying the Forces That Drive Our Spending

It was 1927 and the world was full of exciting new possibilities. Charles Lindbergh had just made the first solo transatlantic flight, and people were starting to view air travel as a viable future option. Lindbergh was instantly famous, and many young aviators began to dream of attempting a similar feat. There were many places airplanes had not gone yet, and young men visualized themselves being the first to fly to exotic, far-off locations.

Just four days after Lindbergh's historic flight, James Dole, the pineapple magnate, offered $25,000 to the first airman to fly from the United States mainland to the island of Hawaii.

This was no small challenge. Hawaii is only a small speck in a vast expanse of water, and aeronautical instruments were still in their infancy. But these facts didn't stop the would-be Lindberghs. Many young men, knowing the odds of actually reaching Hawaii were extremely slim, began a mad rush to be the first. In fact, so many young pilots rose to the contest that James Dole, due to fear that many of these reckless men would lose their lives, changed the rules of the contest to a race on a specific date. His hope was that men would take the time to prepare properly for such a flight.

When the day of the race finally arrived, the first plane lifted off safely, but the second crashed during takeoff. The next one couldn't get off the ground, and three more had immediate mechanical trouble and had to return. Out of fifteen pilots who had signed up for the race, only two actually made it to Hawaii. Over the next eight years, sixteen pilots attempted this flight with eleven successfully landing in Hawaii. Charles Lindbergh himself said, "The flight from California to the Hawaiian Islands was the greatest air feat in history."

Today, flights to Hawaii occur many times a day. Pilots have access to global positioning systems and many other navigational tools that allow them to know exactly where they are at any given time. We can't even comprehend what it would have been like to head out across the Pacific and try to reach the small speck on the map called Hawaii. But why was it so hard to navigate there? A pilot knew where he was taking off from and where he wanted to go. He could take a map, and after locating these two points, easily chart a course. That wasn't difficult. No, the problem wasn't plotting the course; the difficulty was staying on track. Even if he had accurately aimed his aircraft for Honolulu when he left the runway in San Francisco, crosswinds could alter his course without him being aware of it.

So it is with family budgets. Earlier we talked about finding out where we are financially and then deciding where we want to go. Once these two points are identified, we discussed the importance of establishing a budget to get us from where we are to where we want to go. But many of us find ourselves in a position like the pilots trying to fly to Hawaii. We encounter outside influences that greatly affect our finances and threaten to blow us off course.

In this chapter we want to look at some of these influences and try to identify some of the forces that drive our spending.

- Past desires. Recently, while helping a family with their finances, I asked about a particular item which seemed to be consuming a large part of their income. This family really needed every available dollar to go toward consumer debt, but it became apparent that this expense was not up for discussion. This monthly cost involved a recreational activity that the parents had longed to be involved in since they were young, and they were not interested in considering giving it up now. Many of us carry these secret desires from the past. We may wish for a well-decorated home, a gourmet production at every meal, or a certain sport or hobby. But we need to understand that these past longings can greatly influence our finances.

- Fear of the future. Many of us fail to put our trust in the Lord and are fearful about the future. These fears can be very real and can greatly influence our spending. We can easily spend unnecessary money on excessive insurance and survival plans. We need to constantly refocus on the Lord, and our prayer should be like David's when he said, "Preserve me, O God: for in thee do I put my trust."[a]

- Peer pressure and insecurity. What kind of house would you live in if it were invisible to everyone else? What model vehicle would you drive? One major force which tends to blow us off course is the pressure we feel from others. We want to be accepted and we feel the need to live at a certain level to fit in. Sadly, many times this pressure comes from people within our own churches. We feel insecure and fear that if we do not live up to a certain standard, we will not be accepted. It is important to consider the impact this may be having on our spending.

  Different financial advisers have said about Americans, "We buy things we don't need with money we don't have to impress people we don't like." While hopefully the latter is not true of our churches, it is true that we tend to make purchases with an eye toward who will notice. Many of our people are in dire financial straits primarily because of peer pressure.

- Confusing wants and needs. We live in a materialistic age and culture, surrounded daily by items that taste, smell, feel, and look good. Our flesh cries out for all of this. Many of these things can be a blessing to us, but the abundance of options sometimes makes it difficult to discern between our wants and our needs. Marketers have capitalized on

---

[a]Psalm 16:1

this confusion. Just a few years ago the cost of a fountain drink at a fast food restaurant was a small percentage of the price of the meal. Have you checked lately? Recently I looked at the pricing at a local Taco Bell. The price of a Pepsi was almost half that of some of their combos. Once Americans began to view a soft drink as a need, the price was raised and most never noticed. Even if they had noticed, it wouldn't have mattered, because they think of the drink as a legitimate need.

Some of us are having trouble with our budgets because we have confused wants and needs. Many of the items on our shopping lists did not even exist twenty years ago and would not need to be there now. Some of them are time savers, but the fact is that Grandma got along fine without them, and we probably could too.

As those early aviators watched San Francisco disappear behind them, they had very little at their disposal to guide them. The odds were against them, and it would seem that nothing but a remarkable thirst for fame would cause a man to take that kind of risk. It would have been a daunting endeavor even without wind. But ocean winds constantly attempting to blow them off course made it almost impossible.

A pilot had three things back then to help him navigate during an over-water flight. The first was his map and plotted course. As he flew, he constantly referred to the map to determine how close he was staying on course. The second navigational help was the readings he took off the stars and sun. As long as the sky was clear, he could calculate his location by these immovable objects. And last, if he saw a ship on the sea below, he could try contacting it for help in fixing his exact position.

As we consider combating the forces that are constantly trying to derail our vision for Kingdom living, we want to look at these three methods used by early pilots. As we follow the Lord, "contrary winds" can blow strongly, and it will take diligence to stay on track. Consider the following navigational aids as you pursue your vision.

- **Keep the map and course before you.** We have discussed the importance of establishing an overriding vision. Keeping this vision before you is essential if you are going to reach your goal. As you travel, keep coming back to your basic vision. Be sure all your less significant choices line up with your greater decision to live for the Kingdom. Talk about your vision often and remind each other of your goals.

- **Keep examining your position by comparing it to an immovable reference point.** A pilot took readings from the sun and stars as frequently as possible. He never knew when clouds would roll in and obstruct his vision. In the same way, our hold on the immovable Word of God is of extreme importance. Keep examining the teachings of Jesus and use them as reference points. Analyze your current location and direction of travel by His teachings. Many pilots were shocked as they took readings and realized how far they had drifted. Many of us have also been amazed at how quickly we can drift when we begin using the society around us as a reference point. An ongoing analysis of our path in relation to the Word of God is indispensable.

- **Ask for advice and welcome exhortation.** Many pilots were saved because they were willing to ask a passing freighter for its position. It takes a great deal of humility, but many of us who are younger could learn a great deal from the older generation regarding finances if we would just ask. It seems technology has convinced us that the older generation is out of touch. Since many older people have not stayed current with the rapid changes in technology, it is easy to assume we who are younger are smarter. But my experience has been that most who are having difficulty with finances are under forty. Knowing what a megabyte is does not ensure that one has wisdom. If we were a little more willing to ask advice of those who have traveled longer, we would be much more likely to stay on course.

Conclusion

It is not difficult to find out where we are financially, and most of us can set some long-term goals. It takes a little more time to establish a course from where we are to where we want to go. But the major challenge most of us face in reaching our financial goals is staying on track. We can fill out financial statements and create budgets during brief periods of enthusiastic zeal. But the real test comes when we try to implement our vision during the mundane grind of daily life. It is easy to fall back into the same ruts and habits.

But we don't have to fail! If you and your family are united, committed, and willing to communicate with each other, you can succeed. It has been said, "There is a difference between interest and commitment. When you are interested in something, you do it when circumstances are favorable. When you are committed to something, you accept no excuses, only results." Making Christ-centered financial decisions in a self-centered world will take more than just interest. It will require commitment.

Study Questions

1. Share a failure in budgeting. Perhaps you started out with great resolve and then realized months later you had drifted from your vision. What caused this? What did you learn from this?

2. Can you share a time when you made a purchase to buy acceptance?

3. What are some things that were luxuries just a few years ago but are now regarded as needs?

4. Why is a continual study of God's Word so important in helping us maintain our course?

5. How does Malachi 3:16 relate to our tendency to drift? Should we be asking for more personal accountability? Why is this so difficult?

CHAPTER TWENTY-SEVEN
Can We Really Afford to Give?

On November 19, 1854, Sam Houston was baptized into the Rock Creek Church just outside Independence, Texas. Sam was over sixty years old and had earned the reputation of being a coarse and belligerent man. He had lived a hard life, and though his wife had been a believer for years, Sam hadn't felt the need to make such a commitment. Those who knew Sam well said the day of his baptism was a great turning point in his life. Whereas before he had been argumentative and difficult to get along with, after his declaration of faith he became much more gentle and content.

But immediately after Sam's baptism, something else happened which shocked those who knew him well. After the service Sam told the church leaders he would like to start paying half the local minister's monthly salary. When his friends asked him why, Sam's reply was, "My pocketbook was baptized too."

We do not know much about Sam Houston's relationship with the Lord,

> **My pocketbook was baptized too.**

but his statement shows he had one thing right. True conversion will transform every part of a man—right down to his pocketbook. In fact, judging from the number of times Jesus taught about money, we could easily conclude that a man's pocketbook is one of the first places change will occur.

Do We Make Enough to Give?

People in financial trouble tend to ask questions regarding giving and tithing. "In our present financial situation, does the Lord expect us to keep giving?" Before answering this question, I think we should examine a story in the Bible. Perhaps this little account during the life of Jesus can give us some insight into how God views giving. Consider the lesson Jesus taught His disciples as they watched the poor widow give her two mites.

We can imagine what the disciples must have thought. They had heard Jesus say many strange things, but this must have seemed a little ridiculous. "Did you hear what He said?" one of them might have whispered. "Did He really say that poor widow gave more money than the others?"

"Didn't Jesus see how much some of them gave?" another might have added.

Undoubtedly this scene made the disciples scratch their heads, and perhaps we have wondered about it as well. At least we should have. I believe this account provides an invaluable window into the heart of God Himself. Let's look at a few lessons this story provides.

- We can give acceptably regardless of our financial status. This was one more reason the poor heard Jesus gladly. Even the poorest man can please God in his giving. We have all probably entertained the thought at times, "If I had more, I would give more." But this account reveals that, from God's perspective, the most destitute are in an excellent position to give the very most. Every one of us, regardless of our financial situation, is able to give acceptably and please God.

- Proper giving requires abandonment of self. Too often I want to give without giving up any part of my life. I like to give away clothes I am finished using, money that wasn't really allocated for anything anyway, or time that was spare time. But the message in this account is clear. God is looking for abandonment! Are you willing to abandon something in order to give? Can you cheerfully give up something you had planned because God has called you to share? Remember, God's primary interest is in the size of the sacrifice.

- There is a time to forget the bottom line. One of the potential traps in budgeting is to develop a mindset where every decision is made from a bottom-line perspective. "We know there's a real need here, but it's not in the budget." Our decision making can become so mechanical that we hardly hear God's call. But notice the lack of common sense in this widow's decision, yet how Jesus blessed it. It seemed like a crazy thing to do. She just threw her last two mites into the box. What was she going to do now? But sometimes God calls us to places where common sense is a detriment. May we each be sensitive enough to the Spirit to hear when God tells us it is time to forget the bottom line.

- We look at what is given; God looks at what is kept. What was the real difference between the widow and the rich men that day? Surely God was pleased when a rich man threw a large amount of money into the treasury. It took a lot of money to operate the temple, with maintenance on the building, workers to pay, and money to be sent out to the poor. No doubt a temple could burn a lot of money in a month. Those in charge of the treasury were probably thrilled when they saw a wealthy man coming. They may have even wished that some of those old widows would get out of the way. "If the line gets too long," I can hear someone say, "some of our rich men may become discouraged and stay away." But God intently watches something else. While we tend to look at what is given, God's eye has always been on what is kept.

Now let's look again at our original question. "In our present financial situation, does the Lord expect us to keep giving?" This is a question only you can answer before the Lord, but I think there are some questions you should answer before you decide your financial situation precludes giving. As you answer these questions honestly, remember the widow giving her two mites.

- Are you currently spending on any items not needed for survival? If so, could any of these items be abandoned to enable giving?

- If your income suddenly dropped 10 percent, would you survive? If so, is there any reason you couldn't give 10 percent to those in need?

- Do you really believe God is the one providing for your natural needs?

- If those who live around you knew you were failing to give, would they agree there is no way you can?

- More than 80 percent of humanity lives on less than $10 per day, and 30 percent on less than $1 a day.[13] Would you be comfortable explaining to them why you can't share?

- For about $2 we can put a Bible in the hands of someone who is willing to walk miles to study the Word. Would these people understand your reasons for not helping?

There are many more questions we could ask ourselves, and the goal here is not to shame any person living in a developed country. Rather, we want to prayerfully analyze our hearts. Our hearts are extremely deceptive. Are we being honest when we say we can't give? Is it possible we are using the wrong reference point to decide whether or not we can give? Many believers throughout the world are cheerfully and regularly giving even though, from our perspective, they have nothing.

Before we leave this subject, I think it is important to make one clarification. I have worked with individuals who were in such financial straits that I felt they were giving too much. This is very rare, but you might be in a situation where you are not able to give as much as you feel called to without neglecting monthly obligations. I do believe there are situations in which part of our giving can be in acts of service to others. However, this does not mean we should stop giving financially. I have never met anyone yet who was in such dire straits that he could not give some money each month.

How Much Should We Give?

I have been reluctant to say how much should be given. Each of us should answer this question before God. It is important to remember we are stewards, and even though a checking account or piece of property has my name on it, it is not mine. Since I have willingly given every asset I have to God, the question is not how much should I give, but where does God want His assets dispersed?

I have listened to many arguments regarding whether or not the tithe is for us today. For myself, I do not feel I am legally bound to give 10 percent. But I would also confess I have hidden behind this understanding in the past. During our first years of marriage, I would describe our giving habits as sporadic. We gave a little now and then, helped out with someone's misfortune when we could, and sponsored a child or two along the way.

When the issue of tithing came up, I was quick to reply that in our day everything is the Lord's. The Jewish people gave 10 percent to the Lord and then the rest was theirs. I would point out that today everything is owned by God—not just 10 percent. All this was very clear to me. God didn't want legal compliance. He wanted cheerful giving. And some of us in America (thinking primarily of others) should be giving far more than just 10 percent.

But I still remember the chastening of the Spirit when at the end of one year I realized the total amount we gave added up to less than 5 percent of my income. I have talked to many people since that time and have found I am not alone. We all have good intentions, but we find ourselves placing the Kingdom on the back burner. We want to give, but we also want many other things. And somehow this love for other things chokes out our giving and makes us unfruitful. Following are a few pointers that may help you in this area of giving.

- **Give first.** Too often we wait to see if there will be enough left over to give. We fully intend to give, but somehow it doesn't happen. In most of our homes, especially when we are just starting out, we spend whatever is in the checkbook. There are always needs waiting. If charitable giving is as important to you as the rent, it will happen. Financial expert David Bach wrote a book called *Start Late, Finish Rich* to help older people become wealthy. In his book he encourages people who want to be wealthy to pay themselves first. What he is saying is, if you really want to be wealthy when you retire, you need to put your primary emphasis on saving. And the only way to do this effectively is to take money out of each paycheck immediately and make saving your primary focus. If we could only be as dedicated to the Kingdom as our society is to obtaining wealth!

- **Give regularly.** Jonathan Edwards, while he was still a young man, wrote out a list of resolves. His goal was to read over these resolves once a day to assist him in his walk with the Lord, and in his eighteenth resolution he said this: "Resolved, to live so, at all times, as I think is best in my most devout frames, and when I have the clearest notions of the things of the Gospel, and another world."[14]

  Jonathan had found there were times when it was easy to make decisions from an eternal perspective. During these times he clearly felt the guiding of the Holy Spirit. But there were also times when the fog rolled in and his vision was restricted, when eternity wasn't quite as clear and it was easier just to follow his flesh. All of us deal with this, and it is imperative we make decisions on giving when we can sense we are in our most "devout frames" and then keep giving regularly during the times when eternity isn't as clear.

- **Give in love and in the name of Jesus.** Our motives in giving are extremely important. It is possible to give for self-recognition or to appear spiritual. We can give through our church and secretly hope that our congregation will become known for caring for its own. But the Bible is clear that God is looking for a particular type of giving—giving motivated by love and in the name of Jesus and His Kingdom.[a] Examine your motives closely

[a]1 Corinthians 13:3, Mark 9:41, Matthew 10:42

and be sure your only goal is to promote our Lord Jesus and His Kingdom.

- **Give prayerfully and carefully.** Allow the Lord to direct your decisions, and be willing to do some investigation into the needs. In the *Didache,* an early Christian writing, the writer said, "Let thine alms sweat in thy hands till thou know to whom thou shouldst give." In other words, give some thought to where you are giving your money and whom you are helping. Giving is not intended to be a conscience soother. Our goal as stewards is to spend the King's resources in a way that will please the King. If we are serious about that, it seems only logical to ask Him for direction.

- **Give with abandonment.** This is perhaps the most difficult of all for our flesh, but the illustration of the widow with two mites is clear. It thrills the heart of God to see believers who are so sold out to Jesus Christ that they are willing to abandon something for the Kingdom. Those two mites represented the widow's living. They were all she had. But she was willing to give them up for the Kingdom. Analyze your own life. Is there something of value you could give up for the Kingdom? Maybe it is a savings account or some possession that is dear to you. Or perhaps it is a hobby that is using resources that could be redirected. Regardless of what it is, be willing to cheerfully abandon it for the Kingdom, and prove your willingness with action.

- **Have a safe holding place for charitable money.** Many families have benefited from having a separate account for money they are dedicating to giving. When a check comes in, a percentage is placed in this account and viewed as untouchable. This gives opportunity for time and prayer regarding where this money should be given, while protecting it from being sucked into the vortex of daily expenses.

Conclusion

Christians give. It is simply part of being indwelt by the Ultimate Giver. The Apostle Paul, while encouraging the wealthy church at Corinth to share with poor believers in another country, said, "For ye know the grace of our Lord Jesus Christ, that, though he was rich, yet for your sakes he became poor, that ye through his poverty might be rich."[b]

Paul was telling the wealthy believers at Corinth that just as Jesus gave Himself up to share with them, it was their time to share with others.

We are wealthy. Perhaps you don't feel rich, but just the fact that you can read proves you are. A large segment of the world's population cannot afford basic education. Even if you are on welfare in the United States today, you are in the wealthiest 10 percent of the world.

We are rich and have a tremendous opportunity and responsibility to share. A professing believer who does not have within his heart a burning desire to give has either lost, or never had, a vision of what God has done for him. May the Lord help us rekindle that vision and renew a passion for sharing with others.

Study Questions

1. Did it make sense, from a financial point of view, for the widow to give those two mites? What can we learn from this in regard to God's ways and common sense?

2. When can tithing "protect" us from God's call to give more?

3. Why is giving in love and in the name of Jesus so important? Why did Jesus emphasize giving quietly and anonymously?

4. Should we still give even though our motives are not pure? What would happen if we waited until they were?

5. What are some ways, besides giving money, that a family in financial difficulty could give? Are there times a family should refrain from giving money?

[b]2 Corinthians 8:9

CHAPTER TWENTY-EIGHT
Maintaining Focus

Along the back wall of the local paint store is a display rack to assist customers in choosing colors. This type of display is common in paint stores and consists of hundreds, if not thousands, of color samples on narrow cardboard strips. The customer can select several strips, take them home, and discuss the appropriate color for the room with the rest of the family. (Behold how great a matter a few color samples kindleth!)

Something about this rack fascinates me. I study it and marvel at how gradual the changes are between color samples, yet how major the overall change. At the upper left-hand corner of the rack, I find a pure white color sample. Immediately to the right of this is another sample that looks just as white as the first. But if I hold the two samples side by side, I see the second one has a touch of beige mixed in. There is so little change in color I would never notice the difference without good lighting and the first sample for a reference. As I keep moving across the display, this subtle change in color occurs ever so slowly. Finally, when I reach the lower right-hand corner, I see colors with names like charcoal and midnight black.

When I compare the last sample, which is totally black, to the first, which is pure white, the difference is obvious. But throughout the display, as I compare each card to the one beside it, the change is almost indiscernible. Gradually, by adding almost imperceptible changes in color to each card, we have gone from pure white to absolute black.

I tend to avoid these large color displays. There are too many options to choose from, and I am never quite sure I have the one I want.

I prefer to be given ten options so I can choose one and start painting. Once I have chosen my color from among hundreds, how can I be sure the colors on one side or the other wouldn't have been better?

Paint color displays remind me of the financial decisions we must make each day. We are surrounded with a daunting array of choices. Where shall we go? What shall we do? What shall we wear? And what shall we drive? And in each category the array of options seems endless. Sometimes we feel a bit like Christian in *Pilgrim's Progress* as he entered Vanity Fair. We are surrounded by fascinating attractions designed to tempt and entice us. We want to make choices that will help us on our journey to the Celestial City, but we are not always certain how to do this.

On the one hand we have choices that are, like the first paint sample, totally white and pure. We know, for example, it is God's will to assist widows and orphans, so we don't question whether or not we should use our resources for this. On the other hand, there are choices we know are completely wrong because they are in direct violation of the Word of God. We could say those are totally black.

But between black and white are thousands of little options which are neither black nor white. They are somewhere in between. And as we go about each day, sorting through the myriad of options, sometimes we forget about the Celestial City. We get distracted and bogged down and lose sight of the goal.

Let's look at a hypothetical illustration of the type of financial choices we face.

Imagine, for a moment, you are traveling in New York City. It is late in the evening and you need to find a place to eat. There are thousands of restaurants in New York City, and the options range from a basic meal to intemperate gluttony. Imagine all the options laid out before you like an array of paint samples. At the upper left-hand corner you find a restaurant called Gray's Papaya on 402 Avenue. This little shop specializes in providing extremely cheap meals, and you can order their Recession Special, a basic meal with a medium drink, for $2.75.

If you look down at the bottom right-hand corner, you see the world-renowned Masa Restaurant, where evening meals start around $500 per plate. Between these two options is an amazing array of choices. From a Kingdom stewardship point of view, considering how the Lord would want us to use His goods, I think we could all agree on which of the two extremes would be better. Although the cheapest option is not always the healthiest, I do not think the Lord would be displeased if we chose to spend $2.75 at Gray's Papaya for their Recession Special. I hope we could also agree that there are better ways to use our resources than spending over $500 a plate at Masa Restaurant, regardless of how wonderful the food and ambiance. But these are not the only two options. In fact, between these two are thousands of other places where you can purchase a meal.

Vision Creep

One of the problems we deal with in our Christian walk is vision creep. We become convinced of a Biblical truth and are determined to live it out. But as we begin to make the choices required in daily life, we find our vision slowly creeping back toward our flesh and away from our original conviction. Consider again the dining options in New York City. We start in the upper left-hand corner with Gray's Papaya. We want something a little healthier, we reason, so we slowly begin moving across the page toward more expensive options. We begin with a resolve to use God's resources wisely, but as we examine the choices, there is so little difference between options it becomes easier and easier to progress along the scale. Our flesh aids this progression since a shrimp dinner sounds better than teriyaki chicken, and suddenly we realize we have become comfortable spending $25 dollars a plate at a steakhouse. After all, we reason, this is still a long way from paying $500 at Masa Restaurant. But the fact is that there are also many good, healthy options between hotdogs and a steakhouse.

But this illustration is not just about selecting a restaurant. This tendency of vision creep occurs in many areas of our lives. A wealthier man has many more options, and for this reason riches become a great catalyst for vision creep. It happens in our selection of vehicles, clothing, and housing. We start out with a clear vision of using our resources for the Kingdom. But we find ourselves slowly creeping along a progression of choices until we suddenly realize we have strayed from our original vision. This is one of the plagues of affluence, and we greatly underestimate its influence on our lives.

A poor man's options are much simpler. Consider, for a moment, the options of a man who resides in Sudan. He has his own struggles, to be sure, but vision creep in the area of eating probably isn't one of them.

But we don't live in Sudan. So how are we to maintain a godly vision of using our resources for the Kingdom? How can we keep ourselves from slowly moving toward fleshly desires and away from Kingdom building? How can we survive our journey through Vanity Fair?

Drawing Lines for Our Families

One of the ways we can keep our families from the slow, subtle descent toward fleshly desires is to write down some specific things we will or will not do. It is so easy to justify our gradual drift toward materialism. Many times, just like looking at paint samples, there is little difference between options. And if we have not purposed beforehand not to cross a certain line, it is easy to drift. For example, if we have decided in advance not to spend more than $10 for a plate of food, it will greatly simplify our decision making and help us stay on track.

I believe it is important to discuss these decisions as a family. Talk about why you need to draw some personal lines and about the tendency to drift away from God's best. Avoid focusing only on the things you are not going to do and the items you are not going to buy. Keep discussing the places you do want your resources to go. Is there any value in refraining from spending on expensive clothing if the money saved is just going to sit in the bank? Is there any real virtue in driving an older vehicle if the money saved ends up redecorating the living room? The importance of remaining focused on the goal cannot be overstated. All these decisions are purposeless without a guiding spiritual vision.

Possible Scenario

To illustrate one way this can be done, let's imagine a young couple preparing an overriding vision for their family. After spending time in prayer and seeking God's will, they agree to narrow their vision to three basic goals. Their desire is that all their available resources throughout life be funneled into these three primary categories.

- Raise a godly family

- Encourage the saints

- Save the lost

While this is a very basic overriding vision, it gives this young couple a starting point for making smaller choices. As they try to decide other issues, they can always refer to these three primary goals and make sure each smaller choice agrees with one of these goals. But as all of us know, we can justify just about anything to ourselves, and many times, in a weak moment, we make choices that are inconsistent with our original goals.

This young couple understands they have this tendency, so they decide to make some decisions before they find themselves in the heat of the battle. They realize it is more effective to purpose in their hearts, as Daniel did, before the temptation comes. So they take a piece of paper and draw a big circle.

The inside of this circle represents the target. Listed inside are items or activities they feel are consistent with their overriding vision; those listed on the outside represent things they have decided are not aligned with their vision. Let's look at possible discussions which might take place as they categorize their activities or spending.

Expensive Vacations

Unnecessary Home Decorating

Recreational Eating Out

Bass Boat

Encouraging Believers

Maintaining the House

Fishing With Children

Visiting Widows

Helping the Persecuted Church

Inexpensive Vehicles

Amusement Parks

Assisting the Poor

Tent-Camping Equipment

New Vehicles

ATVs, Snowmobiles, Etc.

Recreational Vehicles

"So, what are we going to do about eating out?" the wife asks her husband.

"Well, it is nice to get out of the house once in a while, but since we are trying to give as much as possible, it doesn't seem right to spend twenty-five dollars on a meal when we could eat at home for a fraction of the cost."

"But if we decide not to eat out, what do we do when we are traveling, or what if a friend could use encouragement? Sometimes we meet with friends for breakfast, and that seems to be part of our goal of encouraging the saints."

"Perhaps we should make a distinction between recreational eating and eating somewhere because it fits under one of our primary goals," the husband suggests.

"That sounds reasonable, and I think that would be the most consistent with our overriding vision. But what about stopping for a meal after we've been gone all day and I haven't had time to prepare one?"

"Maybe we should set a dollar amount per meal that we will not exceed in those situations and then try not to let it happen any more than necessary."

The point here is not whether you choose or don't choose to eat in restaurants. The goal is to avoid the slippery slope of vision creep. It is one thing to establish an overriding vision such as raising a godly family, encouraging the saints, and saving the lost. It is not difficult to decide to make choices within those parameters. But the real problem is aligning those little choices with our overriding vision. We set lofty goals and then later realize shamefully that we have drifted back into justifying a lifestyle that is much like an unbeliever's. Agreeing on specifics as a family and writing down our decisions is an effective way to avoid this subtle drift.

Before leaving this topic, one more point is important: These decisions are only for your own family. Nothing in the Word of God specifically says that recreational eating or owning a motor home is sin. Each family needs to focus on its own situation and have much charity for others. A materialistic society is a difficult place to live in, and we do not always know how we would respond if we were in another's shoes. It is easy to frown on another person's choices and have strong convictions against something he has purchased, especially if you can't afford the item anyway. But don't let all this distract you from drawing personal lines for your family. In the materialistic society we live in, I believe this is essential.

The Power of Peer Pressure

Several years ago, during an after-dinner discussion with fellow believers, we were talking about our tendency to spend too much on ourselves. There was some discussion regarding the economic disparity in the world and the fact that we could be doing more to share. At the conclusion of the conversation there was a brief pause, and then a sister who had been listening said, "Well, our family would be willing to live at a lower level if everyone else would too!"

Everyone at the table laughed. Hearing this stated openly sounded funny, and the logic even bordered on the absurd. Why let others dictate your convictions? Yet, as I reflected on the discussion later, she had spoken what most of us were thinking. She was simply being more honest than the rest of us.

We are all aware of areas in our lives where we are being poor stewards, but we don't want to be different. We would like change, but we want to hold hands with others while we do it. We all like to believe we are thinkers. We like to imagine we are charting our own course and independently blazing our own trail. We smile at youth and their tendency to follow each other. If a certain brand of shoe is "cool," they think they must have it. It looks so silly to those of us who are older, and we are sure we have risen above this. But the truth is that most adults are still susceptible to peer pressure. Many of us would be embarrassed if others knew how many poor financial choices we have made based on what others might think. As Isaiah said, we are all like sheep.

Earlier we discussed the powerful influence our self-centered culture has on us, and we looked at ways we can fight this pressure. But sometimes in our Anabaptist settings the most powerful pressure is not coming from without, but from within. We find ourselves making poor financial decisions simply because we are trying to meet the expectations of others within our social circle. And as we succumb to this pressure, we in turn influence others who are watching us.

I wonder sometimes what our homes, vehicles, and many of our daily financial choices would look like if no one were watching. How much are we driven by perceived expectations of others? As your car begins to age, is your primary concern potential repair costs or how driving an older car will affect others' opinions of you? When considering whether to upgrade your living room furniture, what percentage of your decision is based on social pressure? Most of us are swayed by the comments and opinions of others, and we each need to examine our own lives and motives.

Encouraging Community Stewardship

As we have observed among our young people at times, peer pressure is not always negative. Many times youth make good choices simply because others are doing it. In the same way, we can also be influenced in a positive way by the social pressure that surrounds us. With this in mind, it seems important to surround ourselves with brothers and sisters who are serious about Biblical stewardship and willing to live it out in their lives.

So how can we encourage Kingdom values and stewardship in our communities? How can we develop positive peer pressure in our congregations? Let's look at a few ways we can assist in building Biblical values and positive social pressure.

- Be the vision you want to see in others. As we have mentioned, there is a general awareness within our congregations that we could be doing better in this area. But our tight-knit fellowships can

  > **Be the vision you want to see in others.**

  become a hindrance to us and sometimes keep us from following the Spirit's call. We read passages in the Sermon on the Mount and are convicted to make lifestyle changes, but then we fail to change due to fear of others within our fellowship. What would they say, and what kinds of questions might they ask? We allow the fear of man to stifle the Spirit's work in our lives, and meanwhile, our own unwillingness to follow the Lord may be keeping our brother from making lifestyle changes as well. Satan loves this. But imagine how the Lord could use a congregation where each member was willing to live out the stewardship vision God gave him!

- Use times of fellowship to encourage Biblical stewardship. This needs to be done carefully and humbly, but I am convinced that much of our struggle in our congregations is due to our reluctance to discuss topics that matter. We know how to discuss at length subjects that have little eternal value such as weather, farming, business, struggles in other congregations, and the failings of political figures, but seem reluctant to move into crucial topics that affect us daily. In the constant battle against surrounding culture, I need to hear my brother say it is okay to drive an older vehicle. I need to hear discussions that make me thankful for the home I have and create no pressure toward continual improvements. We receive enough pressure from without; let's not allow our times of fellowship to apply additional materialistic pressure from within. If our discussion always centers on landscaping, the latest home decorations, furnishings, or improvements, it will affect the choices we make as families.

- Encourage times of collective teaching on finance and Biblical stewardship. Each of us is in a different setting, but leaders should be encouraged to spend time teaching on this subject. In most of our communities we have good teaching on what we should not do, places we should not visit, and choices we should not make. Many times we focus on what to avoid but neglect to teach the principles behind the practice. For example, many of our churches have taught against flashy colors and stylish designs. But regardless of the color, is spending $35,000 on a personal vehicle consistent with Biblical stewardship? Sometimes the filters we develop to fight against pride and material-ism are effective in one time period but fail to work prop-erly in another. Often this is a result of focusing only on practice and neglecting the principle. It is important that we continually go back to the Word as our source and teach the timeless Biblical principles.

- Encourage godly choices in families around you. Many times our comments unknowingly encourage addition-al spending and consumption. We have been taught to notice, admire, and comment on new dresses, vehicles, fancy desserts, etc. While it is good to bless those around us and "rejoice with those that do rejoice," how often do you commend others in your community for purchasing used clothing, buying a used vehicle, or providing a sim-ple meal when visiting them? Many times our little com-ments are made somewhat thoughtlessly in an attempt to avoid an awkward silence. These comments, which are meant to encourage, have an impact not only on the one we are speaking to but also on bystanders. We all have an opportunity to move our communities closer to a more Scriptural view of using resources by encouraging good choices among us.

Conclusion

We are unquestionably living in a time of unprecedented choices. We have more lifestyle options and ways to feed our flesh than ever before. The paint sample illustration is a daily reality in our lives, and there are thousands of options and corresponding decisions we must make every day. If we are going to avoid being swept along with the prevailing current of materialism and fleshly fulfillment, it will take zeal, dedication to the Word of God, and a passion for holiness in our lives. The effort required to swim against a current is in direct proportion to the power of the current. As the materialistic pressure continues to rise, our generation will need to be more vigilant than earlier generations.

But I am also challenged and encouraged as I observe many of our young people and families. I see a growing desire to be used of the Lord. As I listen to their discussions and watch their lifestyle choices, I am blessed. While my generation spent much time talking about and pursuing "getting ahead," I hear many in the younger generation discussing ways their lives can be useful to the Kingdom. They talk about how to avoid the grip of materialism and the culture of covetousness that surrounds them. May the Lord bless us as we draw lines for our families, encourage separation from the world in a culture of consumerism, and focus our resources on building the Kingdom of Jesus Christ!

Study Questions

1. Have you ever been convicted about something and then found yourself slowly drifting from your original conviction? Share ways vision creep has affected your life.

2. Why does prosperity increase our tendency to stray from our convictions?

3. Why are boundary lines so important for families in our culture? What about lines for our churches?

4. How can we draw lines for our homes while teaching our children not to be judgmental of others?

5. Discuss ways you could encourage good stewardship in your congregation. When is it best to bring up these topics? When is it best to have times of focused teaching?

Chapter Twenty-Nine
The Root of Materialism

T he problem was obvious, but the cause harder to discover. Ideas and opinions spread rampantly, but no one could show any evidence. The only fact everyone could agree on was that hundreds of healthy women were entering hospitals to deliver their children, but dying after becoming infected with what was known as puerperal, or childbed fever. It was the mid-eighteen hundreds, and the established scientific opinion of the day called for bloodletting. Yet the deaths continued. Expectant mothers learned to fear hospitals. In fact, expectant mothers who checked into hospitals had three times the mortality rate of those in midwife wards.

During this time Ignaz Semmelweis, a Hungarian physician, made an important discovery. Ignaz found that almost all cases of puerperal fever could be traced to a lack of cleanliness. To prove his theory, he had all doctors in his hospital begin washing their hands in a chlorinated lime solution each time they left one bedside and went to another. Doctor Semmelweis saw immediate results, and the mortality rate in his hospital dropped dramatically. While this sounds simple and basic in our day, it was so strange and revolutionary in his time that no one would listen. Despite the evidence and Doctor Semmelweis's pleading with other doctors, his findings were largely ignored by the medical community, and bloodletting continued as the approved medical procedure of the day.

History tells us that Doctor Semmelweis, in his passionate attempt to convince his disinterested colleagues, eventually went insane and in 1865 was placed in an asylum, where he died at the age of forty-seven.

He knew that bloodletting and all the various procedures being used at the time would avail nothing as long as doctors kept going from patient to patient spreading disease throughout hospitals. In short, he had found the root cause. The doctors of the day could work long and hard, but the scourge would continue until they dealt with the cause.

In previous chapters we have dealt with many ways believers can fight against the scourge of materialism. We have looked at the importance of tracking our spending, budgeting, and working together as a family. We have talked about the plague of consumer debt and the importance of having an overriding vision for our homes. But it is important to understand that all this is in vain if we fail to address the cause of our problem. So what is the root cause of materialism? Before we look at the source of materialism in believers, let's look at the cause of materialism in the world around us.

Short-Life Theory

I think it is clear why the unbelieving world is in a financial quagmire. It should come as no surprise that the average American family is carrying thousands of dollars in credit card debt and needs two incomes just to stay afloat. Unbelievers view this present life as the main event and death as an end of all things. If you are only going to live seventy years, it is logical to wring as much out of this time as possible. As the saying in the Bible goes, "Eat, drink, and be merry, for tomorrow we die." Perhaps we could call this the short-life theory.

Several years ago I worked with a man who epitomized the short-life theory. His name was Bob, and his father had died suddenly at age fifty-five. His unexpected death made a deep impression on Bob. After his father died, Bob concluded he would probably die young as well, so he decided to live life to the fullest. Bob loved to fish, so he bought a large boat and a big motor home and started going fishing each weekend. To accomplish all this, Bob took out a second mortgage on his home and maxed out his credit cards. After all, he thought, if a man is not going to live long anyway, he may as well live it up while he can.

But Bob's little plan didn't work out as he thought it would. Bob didn't die at fifty-five; in fact, at the time I worked with him, he was around sixty and still in good physical health. He still had his toys but had very little time to play. The debt he had acquired had snowballed, and he needed to work long hours just to keep up with the payments. Bob was a discouraged man. He had lived longer than he had planned.

I can still picture Bob staring bleakly out the window during break time, holding a coffee mug full of beer. Bob's life was nearly over. He didn't believe in an afterlife, and all he could see ahead was living in a deteriorating body, working long hours, and making the consuming monthly payments. Bob had embraced the short-life theory, the foundation of materialism. Materialism is built upon the belief that reality is what a man can touch and feel. The goal of the short-life theory is to grab and possess as much as possible.

We Don't Believe That!

Of course, we do not share Bob's belief that this life is an end in itself. As Christians, we believe in an afterlife. Further, we have publicly stated our willingness to give up this present life for our Lord Jesus Christ. Our focus is on living for Him, and the primary reward we are seeking comes after death. Giving up our claim to fleshly gratification in this life is one of the basic premises for following Christ. Jesus was very clear: every man must decide on which side of the grave he wants to lose his life. Carefully examine these words of Jesus.

> And he that taketh not his cross, and followeth after me, is not worthy of me. He that findeth his life shall lose it: and he that loseth his life for my sake shall find it.[a]

> For whosoever will save his life shall lose it; but whosoever shall lose his life for my sake and the gospel's, the same shall save it. For what shall it profit a man, if he shall gain the whole world, and lose his own soul? Or what shall a man give in exchange for his soul? Whosoever therefore shall be ashamed of me and of my words in this adulterous and sinful generation; of him also shall the Son of man be ashamed, when he cometh in the glory of his Father with the holy angels.[b]

[a]Matthew 10:38-39
[b]Mark 8:35-38

Whosoever shall seek to save his life shall lose it; and whosoever shall lose his life shall preserve it.[c]

These are just a few references in which Jesus explicitly said a man must choose. In fact, this message was so central throughout Jesus' teaching that it is recorded in different ways in each of the Gospels. So what does this message mean?

A Time to Die

Everyone must die. But God has given us a choice. We can choose to live for self in this brief life and die eternally, or we can surrender our lives today and live forever. As we read the words of Jesus, the message is simple and the choice clear: die now or die later.

[c]Luke 17:33

I clearly remember sitting in a house church in China listening to the believers singing "I Have Decided to Follow Jesus." One face in particular is indelibly fixed in my mind. I had listened to this young woman's story the night before—a story that could be told by many first-generation Christians in countries where Christians are persecuted. Through tears she told of coming to believe in Jesus and the cost that had come with her decision. Her parents had been furious, and she had been forced to leave her home and village. She was only about twenty years old, but she chose to walk out with just the clothes she was wearing. Her decision to follow Jesus had cost her everything. Penniless and unable to stay in one place for long, she now traveled through the country working when she could, encouraging other believers, and sharing the Gospel with anyone who would listen.

That morning I listened as they sang, "I have decided to follow Jesus. . . . Though none go with me, still I will follow." I had heard this song many times in the past, but something was different this time. Of course, the language was not familiar, and they sang slower than I was accustomed to, but that wasn't the primary difference. It wasn't the fact that every eye was closed or that tears were coursing down their cheeks as they sang. As I later analyzed what I had observed, I came to this conclusion: the primary difference was this group of believers actually believed and lived what they were singing! These people had actually chosen to give up father and mother and wife and children and brothers and sisters and their own lives also. Their belief in the Gospel and their faith in Jesus Christ were so strong that they had chosen to give up this present life to gain the next. I have been surrounded by what I consider good Christians all my life. I have observed commitment in the lives of those who have instructed and lived close to me. The truth is, however, that most of us have never had to actually walk away from everything to follow Jesus. In fact, most of us have experienced just the opposite. Our families were overjoyed when we chose to follow the Lord. And our friends rejoiced with us. We may have even experienced some pressure to be a part of our church. In one sense, we have never actually had to make a choice. And very subtly we have come to believe we don't need to. We entertain the idea we can have Jesus without giving up our lives.

In the Bible riches sound dangerous, but in our setting wealth doesn't seem quite so scary. Many of the men we admire most are prosperous, even by American standards. Jesus warns very strongly against the pursuit of affluence, but in our circles something is wrong with the man who isn't "getting ahead." Jesus plainly said not to accumulate treasures, yet we quickly label a man inept if he doesn't have much to show for twenty years in business.

How did we get here? How did we move from Jesus' teachings of total abandonment for the Kingdom to wanting more of this world's goods so badly that we will rack up credit card debt to get them? How can it be possible for imitators of Jesus Christ, a man who didn't even own His own bed, to struggle continually with materialism? Why do we continue to chase after the same things our neighbors do? Why do our interests, pursuits, and growing accumulation of goods look so much like the culture around us? What is the root cause of our weakness in this area?

Materialism's Root Cause

I suggest that the root cause of our struggle with materialism is simply unbelief. We know Jesus taught against this mindless pursuit of the materialistic life, yet we don't really believe affluence is that dangerous. We know He taught that a man must choose between seeking fulfillment in this life and seeking the life to come, but somehow we have convinced ourselves there is a third option. We choose to believe the prevailing message of professing Christianity around us rather than the words of Jesus Himself. Our choices expose our unbelief and show we are also entertaining the short-life theory.

Materialism is, by its very nature, a lie. It is the false belief that reality is in that which is seen, and fulfillment is in the accumulation of things around us. It is a belief system and a way of thinking. When Jesus warned against the accumulation of goods, He was not trying to make our lives miserable. He just knew the inherent poverty of earthly wealth and was trying to spare us the ultimate disappointment that comes from chasing it. We read the story of the rich young ruler and marvel that Jesus asked him to give away all he had. But the amazing part of the account of the rich young ruler wasn't how much he had to give up. He was eventually going to lose all his possessions anyway. The stunning part of the story is the priceless opportunity he was given to gain eternal riches.

Our fixation on what he was asked to "give up" exposes our unbelief.

> **Our fixation on what the rich young ruler was asked to "give up" exposes our unbelief.**

Conclusion

God is calling us today to more than just well-balanced financial lives. Many godless people in our society have practical budgets, live disciplined lives, and avoid the scourge of consumer debt. In fact, these attributes describe most successful people in business. But God is calling our families to a higher vision. He is calling us to live for His Kingdom and to use the resources He has given us for His glory. I am convinced that one of the major reasons so many of our homes today are struggling in the area of personal finance is simply a result of unbelief. We have spent too much time admiring and chasing things which have no lasting value and too little time focusing on things of eternal value.

We live in a setting similar to that of Moses in Pharaoh's palace. Just as we are today, he was surrounded with everything a man could want. Every fleshly desire could be met in that palace, yet he willingly gave it all up. The writer of Hebrews said it like this: "By faith Moses, when he was come to years, refused to be called the son of Pharaoh's daughter; choosing rather to suffer affliction with the people of God, than to enjoy the pleasures of sin for a season . . . for he had respect unto the recompense of the reward."[d]

Moses had it all, yet he chose to give it up. He chose rather to give up the present and the things he could see for the future and the unseen. He gave up present pleasure for future reward.

May the same be true in each of our homes. May our lives be so dedicated and consecrated to the building of the Kingdom of the Lord Jesus and so radically different from the surrounding culture that no one will be able to deny that we are choosing Jesus.

[d]Hebrews 11:24-26

Study Questions

1. Why do we tend to forget that a man must choose? Are discipleship and Christian stewardship optional? Can we have all our fleshly wants fulfilled and have Jesus too?

2. We claim that we are following a man who taught His followers not to accumulate wealth, yet we admire those who do. How did we stray this far?

3. Why do our lives and financial goals look so similar to our unbelieving neighbors'?

4. What is the root cause of materialism? How can we more effectively encourage each other to believe and apply what Jesus taught about wealth?

5. How can we encourage each other to focus our lives and resources on building the Kingdom? What are some practical steps we can take?

Endnotes

CHAPTER TWO

[1] Ron Sider, *Rich Christians in an Age of Hunger,* Word Publishing, Dallas, 1997, p. 95.

[2] John de Graaf, David Wann, and Thomas Naylor, *Affluenza,* Berrett-Koehler Publishers, Inc., San Francisco, 2001, p. 24.

CHAPTER THREE

[3] Randy Alcorn, *Money, Possessions, and Eternity,* Tyndale House Publishers, Wheaton, Ill, 1989, p. 185.

[4] Clement of Alexandria, A.D. 190; *The Instructor,* T&T Clark Publishers, Edinburgh, 1869.

CHAPTER TEN

[5] Aaron Lapp, "The Credit Card Crunch," *Calvary Messenger,* April 2008, p. 5.

CHAPTER ELEVEN

[6] Consumer Debt Statistics, <www.money-zine.com/> October 2009.

[7] Laura Craven, "Newark Man Sets Himself on Fire," *New Jersey Star Ledger,* July 30, 2008.

CHAPTER TWELVE

[8] *Sun Herald,* July 13, 2009.

CHAPTER NINETEEN

[9] Orison Swett Marden, *Pushing to the Front,* Thomas Y. Rowell and Company Publishers, New York, 1894, p. 328.

Chapter Twenty-One

[10]Becky Barrow, "Nineteen Minutes—How Long Working Parents Give Their Children," *Daily Mail,* July 19, 2006. (Information quoted from the Office for National Statistics)

Chapter Twenty-Two

[11]John de Graaf, David Wann, and Thomas Naylor, *Affluenza,* Berrett-Koehler Publishers, Inc., San Francisco, 2001, p. 13.

Chapter Twenty-Three

[12]University of Michigan Report, January 7, 2004, Report #CSS04-01.

Chapter Twenty-Seven

[13]Anup Shah, "Poverty Facts & Stats," <www.globalissues.org/> March 28, 2010.

[14]Jonathan Edwards, *The Works of Jonathan Edwards,* Vol. 1, Paternoster-Rowe, London, 1839.

About the Author

Gary Miller has had a growing passion to help Christians use their personal finances to build God's Kingdom. He has also had an interest in working with the poor in Third World countries and started an experimental microloan program in Haiti in an effort to provide aid without creating dependency. As part of this loan program, Gary wrote a teaching manual designed to provide both spiritual and financial teaching.

After Christian Aid Ministries took over this microloan project (SALT Microfinance Solutions), its administrators recognized that the Scriptural principles in Gary's manual were just as pertinent for our American Anabaptist communities, and they asked him to write this book.

Gary was raised in an Anabaptist community in California and lives with his wife Patty and family in the Pacific Northwest. He worked in construction all his life, but now focuses his time and energy on writing and helping find sustainable solutions for the poor.

If you have comments about this book, you can share your thoughts by sending an e-mail to kingdomfinance@camoh.org or writing to Christian Aid Ministries, P.O. Box 360, Berlin, Ohio, 44610.

Christian Aid Ministries

Christian Aid Ministries (CAM) was founded in 1981 as a nonprofit, tax-exempt, 501(c)(3) organization. Our primary purpose is to provide a trustworthy, efficient channel for Amish, Mennonite, and other conservative Anabaptist groups and individuals to minister to physical and spiritual needs around the world.

Annually, CAM distributes approximately fifteen million pounds of food, clothing, medicines, seeds, Bibles, Bible story books, and other Christian literature. Most of the aid goes to needy children, orphans, and Christian families. The main purposes of giving material aid are to help and encourage God's people and to bring the Gospel to a lost and dying world.

CAM's home office is in Berlin, Ohio. In Ephrata, Pennsylvania, CAM has a 55,000 square feet distribution center where food parcels are packed and other relief shipments organized. Next to the distribution center is our meat canning facility. CAM is also associated with seven clothing centers—located in Indiana, Iowa, Illinois, Maryland, Pennsylvania, West Virginia, and Ontario, Canada—where clothing, footwear, comforters, and fabric are received, sorted, and prepared for shipment overseas.

CAM has staff, bases, and distribution networks in Romania, Moldova, Ukraine, Haiti, Nicaragua, Liberia, and Israel. Through our International Crisis (IC) program we also help victims of famine, war, and natural disasters throughout the world. In the USA, volunteers organized under our Disaster Response Services (DRS) program help rebuild in low-income communities devastated by natural disasters such as floods, tornados, and hurricanes. We operate medical clinics in Haiti and Nicaragua.

CAM is controlled by a ten-member board of directors and operated by a five-member executive committee. The organizational structure includes an audit review committee, executive council, ministerial committee, several support committees, and department managers.

CAM is largely a volunteer organization aside from management, supervisory personnel, and bookkeeping operations. Each year, volunteers at our warehouses, field bases, and on Disaster Response Services and International Crisis projects donate more than 200,000 hours.

CAM issues an annual, audited financial statement to its entire mailing list (statements are also available upon request). Fundraising and non-aid administrative expenses are kept as low as possible. Usually these expenses are about one percent of income, which includes cash and donated items in kind.

CAM's ultimate goal is to glorify God and enlarge His kingdom. "... whatsoever ye do, do all to the glory of God." (1 Corinthians 10:31)

For more information or to sign up for CAM's monthly newsletter, please write or call:

Christian Aid Ministries
P.O. Box 360
Berlin, OH 44610
Phone: 330.893.2428
Fax: 330.893.2305

Additional Books

PUBLISHED BY CHRISTIAN AID MINISTRIES

God Knows My Size! / *by Harvey Yoder*
How God answered Silvia Tarniceriu's specific prayer
251 pages $10.99

They Would Not Be Silent / *by Harvey Yoder*
Testimonies of persecuted Christians in Eastern Europe
231 pages $10.99

They Would Not Be Moved / *by Harvey Yoder*
More testimonies of Christians who stood strong under communism
208 pages $10.99

Elena—Strengthened Through Trials / *by Harvey Yoder*
A young Romanian girl strengthened through hardships
240 pages $10.99

Where Little Ones Cry / *by Harvey Yoder*
The sad trails of abandoned children in Liberia during civil war
168 pages plus 16-page picture section $10.99

Wang Ping's Sacrifice / *by Harvey Yoder*
Vividly portrays the house church in China
191 pages $10.99

A Small Price to Pay / *by Harvey Yoder*
Mikhail Khorev's story of suffering under communism
247 pages $10.99

Tsunami!—*from a few that survived* / *by Harvey Yoder*
Survivors tell their stories, some with sorrow and heartbreak, others with
joy and hope.
168 pages $11.99

Tears of the Rain / *by Ruth Ann Stelfox*
Poignantly honest account of a missionary family in war-torn Liberia
479 pages $13.99

A Greater Call / *by Harvey Yoder*
What will it cost Wei to spread the Gospel in China?
195 pages $11.99

Angels in the Night / *by Pablo Yoder*
Pablo Yoder family's experiences in Waslala, Nicaragua
356 pages $12.99

The Happening / *by Harvey Yoder*
Nickel Mines school shooting—healing and forgiveness
173 pages $11.99

In Search of Home / *by Harvey Yoder*
The true story of a Muslim family's miraculous conversion
240 pages $11.99

HeartBridge / *by Johnny Miller*
Joys and sorrows at the Nathaniel Christian Orphanage
272 pages $12.99

The Long Road Home / *by Pablo Yoder*
Will prayers and the Spirit's promptings bring young Pablo "home"?
456 pages $12.99

Miss Nancy / *by Harvey Yoder*
The fascinating story of God's work through the life of an Amish
missionary in Belize
273 pages $11.99

Into Their Hands / *by Harvey Yoder*
Bible smugglers find ingenious ways to transport Bibles into Romania
and the former Soviet Union.
194 pages $11.99

A Heart to Belong / *by Johnny Miller*
A Heart to Belong (sequel to HeartBridge) continues the story of
God's sustaining grace as the Millers love and guide the children of the
Nathaniel Christian Orphanage in Romania.
302 pages $12.99

A Life Redeemed / *by Harvey Yoder*
The inspiring story of Ludlow Walker's journey from his childhood
in Jamacia to his current calling as a minister of the Gospel. An
unforgettable story of God's redeeming grace and transforming power.
232 pages $11.99

Steps to Salvation

The Bible says that we all have "sinned and come short of the glory of God" (Romans 3:23). We sin because we give heed to our sinful nature inherited from Adam's sin in the Garden of Eden, and our sin separates us from God.

God provided the way back to Himself by His only Son, Jesus Christ, who became the spotless Lamb "slain from the foundation of the world." "For God so loved the world that he gave his only begotten Son, that whosoever believeth in him should not perish, but have everlasting life" (John 3:16).

To be reconciled to God and experience life rather than death, and heaven rather than hell (Deuteronomy 30:19), we must repent and believe in the Son of God, the Lord Jesus Christ (Romans 6:32; 6:16).

When we sincerely repent of our sins (Acts 2:38; 3:19; 17:30) and by faith receive Jesus Christ as our Saviour and Lord, God saves us by His grace and we are born again. "That if thou shalt confess with thy mouth the Lord Jesus, and shalt believe in thine heart that God hath raised him from the dead, thou shalt be saved" (Romans 10:9). "For by grace are ye saved through faith; and that not of yourselves: it is the gift of God" (Ephesians 2:8).

When we become born again in Jesus Christ, we become new creatures (2 Corinthians 5:17). We do not continue in sin (1 John 3:9), but give testimony of our new life in Jesus Christ by baptism and obedience to Him. "He that hath my commandments, and keepeth them, he it is that loveth me: and he that loveth me shall be loved of my Father, and I will love him, and will manifest myself to him" (John 14:21).

To grow spiritually, we need to meditate on God's Word and commune with God in prayer. Fellowship with a faithful group of believers is also important to strengthen and maintain our Christian walk (1 John 1:7).